القرآن الكريم

The Holy Quran

جزء عمّ

Juz 'Amma

30th Juz

Arabic Text
With Transliteration
And English Translation

بسم الله الرحمن الرحيم

IN THE NAME OF ALLAH

حازت شرف إصدار هذه الطبعة:

Was awarded the honor of publishing this edition:

دار أبي بن كعب

Dar Ubay Ibn Ka'b

للنشر والتوزيع

for Publishing and Distribution

ISBN: 9798864910948

Instructions

Gh	Th	Dh	Sh
غ	ث	ذ	ش
r Paris in French	three	mother	sh
a	i	u	'
ـَ	ـِ	ـُ	ء
but	bit	put	a
Ş ş	Đ đ	Ţ ţ	q
ص	ض	ط	ق
bus	dull	tumble	car
Ā ā	Ī ī	Ū ū	á
ـَا	ـِي	ـُو	ى
bad	beat	fruit	the
`	Say a-a-a-ah and try to raise the lower part of your throat in order to narrow the passage through which the air is expelled.		
ع			
Ĥ ĥ	Produced by expelling the air through a narrowed throat in much the same way as when one tries to clear one's throat.		
ح			
Ž ž	Start with the th sound in mother, then raise your tongue as much possible to produce the ž.		
ظ			
kh	The sound of ch in Scottish loch, but rougher.		
خ			

سُورَةُ الفَاتِحَة

THE OPENER 1 Al-Fatihah

Bismi Al-Lahi Ar-Raĥmāni Ar-Raĥīmi	(1) In the name of Allāh, the Entirely Merciful, the Especially Merciful.	بِسۡمِ ٱللَّهِ ٱلرَّحۡمَٰنِ ٱلرَّحِيمِ ١
Al-Ĥamdu Lillahi Rabbi Al-`Ālamīna	(2) [All] praise is [due] to Allāh, Lord of the worlds -	ٱلۡحَمۡدُ لِلَّهِ رَبِّ ٱلۡعَٰلَمِينَ ٢
Ar-Raĥmāni Ar-Raĥīmi	(3) The Entirely Merciful, the Especially Merciful,	ٱلرَّحۡمَٰنِ ٱلرَّحِيمِ ٣
Māliki Yawmi Ad-Dīni !!	(4) Sovereign of the Day of Recompense.	مَٰلِكِ يَوۡمِ ٱلدِّينِ ٤
'Īyāka Na`budu Wa 'Īyāka Nasta`īnu	(5) It is You we worship and You we ask for help.	إِيَّاكَ نَعۡبُدُ وَإِيَّاكَ نَسۡتَعِينُ ٥
Ahdinā Aş-Şirāţa Al-Mustaqīma	(6) Guide us to the straight path -	ٱهۡدِنَا ٱلصِّرَٰطَ ٱلۡمُسۡتَقِيمَ ٦
Şirāţa Al-Ladhīna 'An`amta `Alayhim Ghayri Al-Maghđūbi `Alayhim Wa Lā Ađ-Đāllīna	(7) The path of those upon whom You have bestowed favor, not of those who have earned [Your] anger or of those who are astray.	صِرَٰطَ ٱلَّذِينَ أَنۡعَمۡتَ عَلَيۡهِمۡ غَيۡرِ ٱلۡمَغۡضُوبِ عَلَيۡهِمۡ وَلَا ٱلضَّآلِّينَ ٧

سُورَةُ النَّبَإِ

THE TIDINGS ٧٨ An-Naba

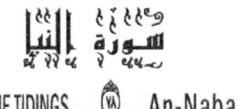

Bismi Al-Lahi Ar-Raĥmāni Ar-Raĥīmi	In the name of Allāh, the Entirely Merciful, the Especially Merciful.	بِسۡمِ ٱللَّهِ ٱلرَّحۡمَٰنِ ٱلرَّحِيمِ
\`Amma Yatasā'alūna	(1) About what are they asking one another?	عَمَّ يَتَسَآءَلُونَ ١
\`Ani An-Naba'i Al-\`Ažīmi	(2) About the great news	عَنِ ٱلنَّبَإِ ٱلۡعَظِيمِ ٢
Al-La<u>dh</u>ī Hum Fīhi Mu<u>kh</u>talifūna	(3) That over which they are in disagreement.	ٱلَّذِي هُمۡ فِيهِ مُخۡتَلِفُونَ ٣
Kallā Saya\`lamūna	(4) No! They are going to know.	كَلَّا سَيَعۡلَمُونَ ٤
<u>Th</u>umma Kallā Saya\`lamūna	(5) Then, no! They are going to know.	ثُمَّ كَلَّا سَيَعۡلَمُونَ ٥
'Alam Naj\`ali Al-'Arđa Mihādāan	(6) Have We not made the earth a resting place?	أَلَمۡ نَجۡعَلِ ٱلۡأَرۡضَ مِهَٰدٗا ٦
Wa Al-Jibāla 'Awtādāan	(7) And the mountains as stakes?	وَٱلۡجِبَالَ أَوۡتَادٗا ٧

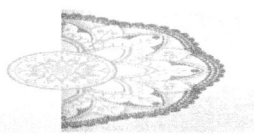

Wa Khalaqnākum 'Azwājāan	(8) And We created you in pairs.	وَخَلَقْنَٰكُمْ أَزْوَٰجًا ٨
Wa Ja`alnā Nawmakum Subātāan	(9) And made your sleep [a means for] rest	وَجَعَلْنَا نَوْمَكُمْ سُبَاتًا ٩
Wa Ja`alnā Al-Layla Libāsāan	(10) And made the night as clothing.	وَجَعَلْنَا ٱلَّيْلَ لِبَاسًا ١٠
Wa Ja`alnā An-Nahāra Ma`āshāan	(11) And made the day for livelihood.	وَجَعَلْنَا ٱلنَّهَارَ مَعَاشًا ١١
Wa Banaynā Fawqakum Sab`āan Shidādāan	(12) And constructed above you seven strong [heavens].	وَبَنَيْنَا فَوْقَكُمْ سَبْعًا شِدَادًا ١٢
Wa Ja`alnā Sirājāan Wa Hhājāan	(13) And made [therein] a burning lamp	وَجَعَلْنَا سِرَاجًا وَهَّاجًا ١٣
Wa 'Anzalnā Mina Al-Mu`şirāti Mā'an Thajjājāan	(14) And sent down, from the rain clouds, pouring water.	وَأَنزَلْنَا مِنَ ٱلْمُعْصِرَٰتِ مَآءً ثَجَّاجًا ١٤
Linukhrija Bihi Ĥabbāan Wa Nabātāan	(15) That We may bring forth thereby grain and vegetation.	لِّنُخْرِجَ بِهِۦ حَبًّا وَنَبَاتًا ١٥

Wa Jannātin 'Alfāfāan	(16) And gardens of entwined growth.	وَجَنَّـٰتٍ أَلْفَافًا ﴿١٦﴾
'Inna Yawma Al-Faşli Kāna Mīqātāan	(17) Indeed, the Day of Judgement is an appointed time -	إِنَّ يَوْمَ ٱلْفَصْلِ كَانَ مِيقَـٰتًا ﴿١٧﴾
Yawma Yunfakhu Fī Aş-Şūri Fata'tūna 'Afwājāan	(18) The Day the Horn is blown and you will come forth in multitudes	يَوْمَ يُنفَخُ فِى ٱلصُّورِ فَتَأْتُونَ أَفْوَاجًا ﴿١٨﴾
Wa Futiĥati As-Samā'u Fakānat 'Abwābāan	(19) And the heaven is opened and will become gateways.	وَفُتِحَتِ ٱلسَّمَآءُ فَكَانَتْ أَبْوَٰبًا ﴿١٩﴾
Wa Suyyirati Al-Jibālu Fakānat Sarābāan	(20) And the mountains are removed and will be [but] a mirage.	وَسُيِّرَتِ ٱلْجِبَالُ فَكَانَتْ سَرَابًا ﴿٢٠﴾
'Inna Jahannama Kānat Mirşādāan	(21) Indeed, Hell has been lying in wait	إِنَّ جَهَنَّمَ كَانَتْ مِرْصَادًا ﴿٢١﴾
Lilţţāghīna Ma'ābāan	(22) For the transgressors, a place of return,	لِّلطَّـٰغِينَ مَـَٔابًا ﴿٢٢﴾
Lābithīna Fīhā 'Aĥqābāan	(23) In which they will remain for ages [unending].	لَّـٰبِثِينَ فِيهَآ أَحْقَابًا ﴿٢٣﴾

Lā Yadhūqūna Fīhā Bardāan Wa Lā Sharābāan	(24) They will not taste therein [any] coolness or drink.	لَّا يَذُوقُونَ فِيهَا بَرْدًا وَلَا شَرَابًا ﴿٢٤﴾
'Illā Ĥamīmāan Wa Ghassāqāan	(25) Except scalding water and [foul] purulence -	إِلَّا حَمِيمًا وَغَسَّاقًا ﴿٢٥﴾
Jazā'an Wifāqāan	(26) An appropriate recompense.	جَزَآءً وِفَاقًا ﴿٢٦﴾
'Innahum Kānū Lā Yarjūna Ĥisābāan	(27) Indeed, they were not expecting an account	إِنَّهُمْ كَانُوا۟ لَا يَرْجُونَ حِسَابًا ﴿٢٧﴾
Wa Kadhdhabū Bi'āyātinā Kidhdhābāan	(28) And denied Our verses with [emphatic] denial.	وَكَذَّبُوا۟ بِـَٔايَـٰتِنَا كِذَّابًا ﴿٢٨﴾
Wa Kulla Shay'in 'Aĥşaynāhu Kitābāan	(29) But all things We have enumerated in writing.	وَكُلَّ شَىْءٍ أَحْصَيْنَـٰهُ كِتَـٰبًا ﴿٢٩﴾
Fadhūqū Falan Nazīdakum 'Illā `Adhābāan	(30) "So taste [the penalty], and never will We increase you except in torment."	فَذُوقُوا۟ فَلَن نَّزِيدَكُمْ إِلَّا عَذَابًا ﴿٣٠﴾
'Inna Lilmuttaqīna Mafāzāan	(31) Indeed, for the righteous is attainment	إِنَّ لِلْمُتَّقِينَ مَفَازًا ﴿٣١﴾
Ĥadā'iqa Wa 'A`nābāan	(32) Gardens and grapevines.	حَدَآئِقَ وَأَعْنَـٰبًا ﴿٣٢﴾

Wa Kawā`iba 'Atrābāan	(33) And full-breasted [companions] of equal age.	وَكَوَاعِبَ أَتۡرَابٗا ٣٣
Wa Ka'sāan Dihāqāan	(34) And a full cup.	وَكَأۡسٗا دِهَاقٗا ٣٤
Lā Yasma`ūna Fīhā Laghwan Wa Lā Kidhdhābāan	(35) No ill speech will they hear therein or any falsehood -	لَّا يَسۡمَعُونَ فِيهَا لَغۡوٗا وَلَا كِذَّٰبٗا ٣٥
Jazā'an Min Rabbika `Aţā'an Ĥisābāan	(36) [As] reward from your Lord, [a generous] gift [made due by] account,	جَزَآءٗ مِّن رَّبِّكَ عَطَآءً حِسَابٗا ٣٦
Rabbi As-Samāwāti Wa Al-'Arđi Wa Mā Baynahumā Ar-Raĥmāni Lā Yamlikūna Minhu Khiţābāan	(37) [From] the Lord of the heavens and the earth and whatever is between them, the Most Merciful. They possess not from Him [authority for] speech.	رَّبِّ ٱلسَّمَٰوَٰتِ وَٱلۡأَرۡضِ وَمَا بَيۡنَهُمَا ٱلرَّحۡمَٰنِۖ لَا يَمۡلِكُونَ مِنۡهُ خِطَابٗا ٣٧
Yawma Yaqūmu Ar-Rūĥu Wa Al-Malā'ikatu Şaffāan Lā Yatakallamūna 'Illā Man 'Adhina Lahu Ar-Raĥmānu Wa Qāla Şawābāan	(38) The Day that the Spirit [i.e., Gabriel] and the angels will stand in rows, they will not speak except for one whom the Most Merciful permits, and he will say what is correct.	يَوۡمَ يَقُومُ ٱلرُّوحُ وَٱلۡمَلَٰٓئِكَةُ صَفّٗاۖ لَّا يَتَكَلَّمُونَ إِلَّا مَنۡ أَذِنَ لَهُ ٱلرَّحۡمَٰنُ وَقَالَ صَوَابٗا ٣٨

Dhālika Al-Yawmu Al-Ĥaqqu Faman Shā'a Attakhadha 'Ilá Rabbihi Ma'ābāan	(39) That is the True [i.e., certain] Day; so he who wills may take to his Lord a [way of] return.	ذَٰلِكَ ٱلۡيَوۡمُ ٱلۡحَقُّۖ فَمَن شَآءَ ٱتَّخَذَ إِلَىٰ رَبِّهِۦ مَـَٔابًا ٣٩
'Innā 'Andharnākum `Adhābāan Qarībāan Yawma Yanžuru Al-Mar'u Mā Qaddamat Yadāhu Wa Yaqūlu Al-Kāfiru Yā Laytanī Kuntu Turābāan	(40) Indeed, We have warned you of an impending punishment on the Day when a man will observe what his hands have put forth and the disbeliever will say, "Oh, I wish that I were dust!"	إِنَّآ أَنذَرۡنَٰكُمۡ عَذَابٗا قَرِيبٗا يَوۡمَ يَنظُرُ ٱلۡمَرۡءُ مَا قَدَّمَتۡ يَدَاهُ وَيَقُولُ ٱلۡكَافِرُ يَٰلَيۡتَنِي كُنتُ تُرَٰبَۢا ٤٠

سورة النازعات

THOSE WHO DRAG FORTH ٧٩ An-Nazi'at

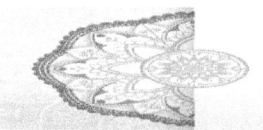

Bismi Al-Lahi Ar-Raĥmāni Ar-Raĥīmi	In the name of Allāh, the Entirely Merciful, the Especially Merciful.	بِسۡمِ ٱللَّهِ ٱلرَّحۡمَٰنِ ٱلرَّحِيمِ
Wa An-Nāzi`āti Gharqāan	(1) By those [angels] who extract with violence	وَٱلنَّٰزِعَٰتِ غَرۡقٗا ١

Wa An-Nāshiţāti Nashţāan	(2) And [by] those who remove with ease	وَٱلنَّٰشِطَٰتِ نَشۡطٗا ٢
Wa As-Sābiĥāti Sabĥāan	(3) And [by] those who glide [as if] swimming	وَٱلسَّٰبِحَٰتِ سَبۡحٗا ٣
Fālssābiqāti Sabqāan	(4) And those who race each other in a race	فَٱلسَّٰبِقَٰتِ سَبۡقٗا ٤
Fālmudabbirāti 'Amrāan	(5) And those who arrange [each] matter,	فَٱلۡمُدَبِّرَٰتِ أَمۡرٗا ٥
Yawma Tarjufu Ar-Rājifah(tu)	(6) On the Day the blast [of the Horn] will convulse [creation],	يَوۡمَ تَرۡجُفُ ٱلرَّاجِفَةُ ٦
Tatba`uhā Ar-Rādifah(tu)	(7) There will follow it the subsequent [one].	تَتۡبَعُهَا ٱلرَّادِفَةُ ٧
Qulūbun Yawma'idhin Wājifah(tun)	(8) Hearts, that Day, will tremble,	قُلُوبٞ يَوۡمَئِذٖ وَاجِفَةٌ ٨
'Abşāruhā Khāshi`ah(tun)	(9) Their eyes humbled.	أَبۡصَٰرُهَا خَٰشِعَةٞ ٩
Yaqūlūna 'A'innā Lamardūdūna Fī Al-Ĥāfirah(ti)	(10) They are [presently] saying, "Will we indeed be returned to [our] former state [of life]?	يَقُولُونَ أَءِنَّا لَمَرۡدُودُونَ فِي ٱلۡحَافِرَةِ ١٠

'A'idhā Kunnā `Ižāmāan Nakhirah(tan)	(11) Even if we should be decayed bones?"	أَءِذَا كُنَّا عِظَٰمًا نَّخِرَةً ﴿١١﴾
Qālū Tilka 'Idhāan Karratun Khāsirah(tun)	(12) They say, "That, then, would be a losing return."	قَالُواْ تِلْكَ إِذًا كَرَّةٌ خَاسِرَةٌ ﴿١٢﴾
Fa'innamā Hiya Zajratun Wāĥidah(tun)	(13) Indeed, it will be but one shout,	فَإِنَّمَا هِيَ زَجْرَةٌ وَٰحِدَةٌ ﴿١٣﴾
Fa'idhā Hum Bis-Sāhirah(ti)	(14) And suddenly they will be [alert] upon the earth's surface.	فَإِذَا هُم بِٱلسَّاهِرَةِ ﴿١٤﴾
Hal 'Tāka Ĥadīthu Mūsá	(15) Has there reached you the story of Moses? -	هَلْ أَتَىٰكَ حَدِيثُ مُوسَىٰٓ ﴿١٥﴾
'Idh Nādāhu Rabbuhu Bil-Wādi Al-Muqaddasi Ţūáan	(16) When his Lord called to him in the sacred valley of Ţuwā,	إِذْ نَادَىٰهُ رَبُّهُۥ بِٱلْوَادِ ٱلْمُقَدَّسِ طُوًى ﴿١٦﴾
Adh/hab 'Ilá Fir`awna 'Innahu Ţaghá	(17) "Go to Pharaoh. Indeed, he has transgressed.	ٱذْهَبْ إِلَىٰ فِرْعَوْنَ إِنَّهُۥ طَغَىٰ ﴿١٧﴾
Faqul Hal Laka 'Ilá 'An Tazakká	(18) And say to him, 'Would you [be willing to] purify yourself	فَقُلْ هَل لَّكَ إِلَىٰٓ أَن تَزَكَّىٰ ﴿١٨﴾

Wa 'Ahdiyaka 'Ilá Rabbika Fatakhshá	(19) And let me guide you to your Lord so you would fear [Him]?'"	وَأَهۡدِيَكَ إِلَىٰ رَبِّكَ فَتَخۡشَىٰ ١٩
Fa'arāhu Al-'Āyata Al-Kubrá	(20) And he showed him the greatest sign,	فَأَرَىٰهُ ٱلۡأٓيَةَ ٱلۡكُبۡرَىٰ ٢٠
Fakadhdhaba Wa `Aşá	(21) But he [i.e., Pharaoh] denied and disobeyed.	فَكَذَّبَ وَعَصَىٰ ٢١
Thumma 'Adbara Yas`á	(22) Then he turned his back, striving [i.e., plotting].	ثُمَّ أَدۡبَرَ يَسۡعَىٰ ٢٢
Fahashara Fanādá	(23) And he gathered [his people] and called out.	فَحَشَرَ فَنَادَىٰ ٢٣
Faqāla 'Anā Rabbukumu Al-'A`lá	(24) And said, "I am your most exalted lord."	فَقَالَ أَنَا۠ رَبُّكُمُ ٱلۡأَعۡلَىٰ ٢٤
Fa'akhadhahu Al-Lahu Nakāla Al-'Ākhirati Wa Al-'Ūlá	(25) So Allāh seized him in exemplary punishment for the last and the first [transgression]..	فَأَخَذَهُ ٱللَّهُ نَكَالَ ٱلۡأٓخِرَةِ وَٱلۡأُولَىٰٓ ٢٥
'Inna Fī Dhālika La`ibratan Liman Yakhshá	(26) Indeed in that is a lesson [i.e., warning] for whoever would fear [Allāh].	إِنَّ فِي ذَٰلِكَ لَعِبۡرَةٗ لِّمَن يَخۡشَىٰٓ ٢٦

'A'antum 'Ashaddu Khalqāan 'Ami As-Samā'u Banāhā	(27) Are you a more difficult creation or is the heaven? He [i.e., Allāh] constructed it.	ءَأَنتُمْ أَشَدُّ خَلْقًا أَمِ ٱلسَّمَآءُ ۚ بَنَىٰهَا ﴿٢٧﴾
Rafa`a Samkahā Fasawwāhā	(28) He raised its ceiling and proportioned it.	رَفَعَ سَمْكَهَا فَسَوَّىٰهَا ﴿٢٨﴾
Wa 'Aghţasha Laylahā Wa 'Akhraja Đuĥāhā	(29) And He darkened its night and extracted its brightness.	وَأَغْطَشَ لَيْلَهَا وَأَخْرَجَ ضُحَىٰهَا ﴿٢٩﴾
Wa Al-'Arđa Ba`da Dhālika Daĥāhā	(30) And after that He spread the earth.	وَٱلْأَرْضَ بَعْدَ ذَٰلِكَ دَحَىٰهَآ ﴿٣٠﴾
'Akhraja Minhā Mā'ahā Wa Mar`āhā	(31) He extracted from it its water and its pasture,	أَخْرَجَ مِنْهَا مَآءَهَا وَمَرْعَىٰهَا ﴿٣١﴾
Wa Al-Jibāla 'Arsāhā	(32) And the mountains He set firmly	وَٱلْجِبَالَ أَرْسَىٰهَا ﴿٣٢﴾
Matā`āan Lakum Wa Li'an`āmikum	(33) As enjoyment [i.e., provision] for you and your grazing livestock.	مَتَٰعًا لَّكُمْ وَلِأَنْعَٰمِكُمْ ﴿٣٣﴾
Fa'idhā Jā'ati Aţ-Ţāmmatu Al-Kubrá	(34) But when there comes the greatest Overwhelming Calamity -	فَإِذَا جَآءَتِ ٱلطَّآمَّةُ ٱلْكُبْرَىٰ ﴿٣٤﴾

Yawma Yatadhakkaru Al-'Insānu Mā Sa`á	(35) The Day when man will remember that for which he strove,	يَوْمَ يَتَذَكَّرُ ٱلْإِنسَٰنُ مَا سَعَىٰ ٣٥
Wa Burrizati Al-Jaĥīmu Liman Yará	(36) And Hellfire will be exposed for [all] those who see -	وَبُرِّزَتِ ٱلْجَحِيمُ لِمَن يَرَىٰ ٣٦
Fa'ammā Man Ţaghá	(37) So as for he who transgressed	فَأَمَّا مَن طَغَىٰ ٣٧
Wa 'Āthara Al-Ĥayāata Ad-Dunyā	(38) And preferred the life of the world,	وَءَاثَرَ ٱلْحَيَوٰةَ ٱلدُّنْيَا ٣٨
Fa'inna Al-Jaĥīma Hiya Al-Ma'wá	(39) Then indeed, Hellfire will be [his] refuge.	فَإِنَّ ٱلْجَحِيمَ هِىَ ٱلْمَأْوَىٰ ٣٩
Wa 'Ammā Man Khāfa Maqāma Rabbihi Wa Nahá An-Nafsa `Ani Al-Hawá	(40) But as for he who feared the position of his Lord and prevented the soul from [unlawful] inclination,	وَأَمَّا مَنْ خَافَ مَقَامَ رَبِّهِۦ وَنَهَى ٱلنَّفْسَ عَنِ ٱلْهَوَىٰ ٤٠
Fa'inna Al-Jannata Hiya Al-Ma'wá	(41) Then indeed, Paradise will be [his] refuge.	فَإِنَّ ٱلْجَنَّةَ هِىَ ٱلْمَأْوَىٰ ٤١
Yas'alūnaka `Ani As-Sā`ati 'Ayyāna Mursāhā	(42) They ask you, [O Muĥammad], about the Hour: when is its arrival?	يَسْـَٔلُونَكَ عَنِ ٱلسَّاعَةِ أَيَّانَ مُرْسَىٰهَا ٤٢

Fīma 'Anta Min Dhikrāhā	(43) In what [position] are you that you should mention it?	فِيمَ أَنتَ مِن ذِكۡرَىٰهَآ ٤٣
'Ilá Rabbika Muntahāhā	(44) To your Lord is its finality.	إِلَىٰ رَبِّكَ مُنتَهَىٰهَآ ٤٤
'Innamā 'Anta Mundhiru Man Yakhshāhā	(45) You are only a warner for those who fear it.	إِنَّمَآ أَنتَ مُنذِرُ مَن يَخۡشَىٰهَا ٤٥
Ka'annahum Yawma Yarawnahā Lam Yalbathū 'Illā `Ashīyatan 'Aw Đuĥāhā	(46) It will be, on the Day they see it, as though they had not remained [in the world] except for an afternoon or a morning thereof.	كَأَنَّهُمۡ يَوۡمَ يَرَوۡنَهَا لَمۡ يَلۡبَثُوٓاْ إِلَّا عَشِيَّةً أَوۡ ضُحَىٰهَا ٤٦

سورة عبس

HE FROWNED ٨ 'Abasa

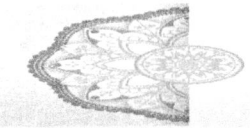

Bismi Al-Lahi Ar-Raĥmāni Ar-Raĥīmi	In the name of Allāh, the Entirely Merciful, the Especially Merciful.	بِسۡمِ ٱللَّهِ ٱلرَّحۡمَٰنِ ٱلرَّحِيمِ
`Abasa Wa Tawallá	(1) He [i.e., the Prophet (ﷺ)] frowned and turned away	عَبَسَ وَتَوَلَّىٰٓ ١

'An Jā'ahu Al-'A`má	(2) Because there came to him the blind man, [interrupting].	أَن جَآءَهُ ٱلْأَعْمَىٰ ٢
Wa Mā Yudrīka La`allahu Yazzakká	(3) But what would make you perceive, [O Muḥammad], that perhaps he might be purified	وَمَا يُدْرِيكَ لَعَلَّهُۥ يَزَّكَّىٰٓ ٣
'Aw Ya<u>dhdh</u>akkaru Fatanfa`ahu A<u>dh</u>-<u>Dh</u>ikrá	(4) Or be reminded and the remembrance would benefit him?	أَوْ يَذَّكَّرُ فَتَنفَعَهُ ٱلذِّكْرَىٰٓ ٤
'Ammā Mani <u>A</u>sta<u>gh</u>ná	(5) As for he who thinks himself without need,	أَمَّا مَنِ ٱسْتَغْنَىٰ ٥
Fa'anta Lahu Taṣaddá	(6) To him you give attention.	فَأَنتَ لَهُۥ تَصَدَّىٰ ٦
Wa Mā `Alayka 'Allā Yazzakká	(7) And not upon you [is any blame] if he will not be purified.	وَمَا عَلَيْكَ أَلَّا يَزَّكَّىٰ ٧
Wa 'Ammā Man Jā'aka Yas`á	(8) But as for he who came to you striving [for knowledge]	وَأَمَّا مَن جَآءَكَ يَسْعَىٰ ٨
Wa Huwa Ya<u>khsh</u>á	(9) While he fears [Allāh],	وَهُوَ يَخْشَىٰ ٩

Fa'anta `Anhu Talahhá	(10) From him you are distracted.	فَأَنتَ عَنۡهُ تَلَهَّىٰ ١٠
Kallā 'Innahā Tadhkirah(tun)	(11) No! Indeed, they [i.e., these verses] are a reminder;	كَلَّآ إِنَّهَا تَذۡكِرَةٞ ١١
Faman Shā'a Dhakarahu	(12) So whoever wills may remember it.	فَمَن شَآءَ ذَكَرَهُۥ ١٢
Fī Şuhufin Mukarramah(tin)	(13) [It is recorded] in honored sheets,	فِي صُحُفٖ مُّكَرَّمَةٖ ١٣
Marfū`atin Muţahharah(tin)	(14) Exalted and purified,	مَّرۡفُوعَةٖ مُّطَهَّرَةِۭ ١٤
Bi'aydī Safarah(tin)	(15) [Carried] by the hands of messenger-angels,	بِأَيۡدِي سَفَرَةٖ ١٥
Kirāmin Bararah(tin)	(16) Noble and dutiful.	كِرَامِۭ بَرَرَةٖ ١٦
Qutila Al-'Insānu Mā 'Akfarahu	(17) Destroyed [i.e., cursed] is man; how disbelieving is he.	قُتِلَ ٱلۡإِنسَٰنُ مَآ أَكۡفَرَهُۥ ١٧
Min 'Ayyi Shay'in Khalaqahu	(18) From what thing [i.e., substance] did He create him?	مِنۡ أَيِّ شَيۡءٍ خَلَقَهُۥ ١٨
Min Nuţfatin Khalaqahu Faqaddarahu	(19) From a sperm-drop He created him and destined for him;	مِن نُّطۡفَةٍ خَلَقَهُۥ فَقَدَّرَهُۥ ١٩

Thumma As-Sabīla Yassarahu	(20) Then He eased the way for him;	ثُمَّ ٱلسَّبِيلَ يَسَّرَهُۥ ﴿٢٠﴾
Thumma 'Amātahu Fa'aqbarahu	(21) Then He causes his death and provides a grave for him.	ثُمَّ أَمَاتَهُۥ فَأَقْبَرَهُۥ ﴿٢١﴾
Thumma 'Idhā Shā'a 'Ansharahu	(22) Then when He wills, He will resurrect him.	ثُمَّ إِذَا شَآءَ أَنشَرَهُۥ ﴿٢٢﴾
Kallā Lammā Yaqđi Mā 'Amarahu	(23) No! He [i.e., man] has not yet accomplished what He commanded him.	كَلَّا لَمَّا يَقْضِ مَآ أَمَرَهُۥ ﴿٢٣﴾
Falyanžuri Al-'Insānu 'Ilá Ța`āmihi	(24) Then let mankind look at his food -	فَلْيَنظُرِ ٱلْإِنسَٰنُ إِلَىٰ طَعَامِهِۦٓ ﴿٢٤﴾
'Annā Şababnā Al-Mā'a Şabbāan	(25) How We poured down water in torrents,	أَنَّا صَبَبْنَا ٱلْمَآءَ صَبًّا ﴿٢٥﴾
Thumma Shaqaqnā Al-'Arđa Shaqqāan	(26) Then We broke open the earth, splitting [it with sprouts],	ثُمَّ شَقَقْنَا ٱلْأَرْضَ شَقًّا ﴿٢٦﴾
Fa'anbatnā Fīhā Ĥabbāan	(27) And caused to grow within it grain	فَأَنۢبَتْنَا فِيهَا حَبًّا ﴿٢٧﴾
Wa `Inabāan Wa Qađbāan	(28) And grapes and herbage	وَعِنَبًا وَقَضْبًا ﴿٢٨﴾

Wa Zaytūnāan Wa Nakhlāan	(29) And olive and palm trees	وَزَيۡتُونٗا وَنَخۡلٗا ٢٩
Wa Ĥadā'iqa Ghulbāan	(30) And gardens of dense shrubbery	وَحَدَآئِقَ غُلۡبٗا ٣٠
Wa Fākihatan Wa 'Abbāan	(31) And fruit and grass -	وَفَٰكِهَةٗ وَأَبّٗا ٣١
Matā`āan Lakum Wa Li'an`āmikum	(32) [As] enjoyment [i.e., provision] for you and your grazing livestock.	مَّتَٰعٗا لَّكُمۡ وَلِأَنۡعَٰمِكُمۡ ٣٢
Fa'idhā Jā'ati Aş-Şākhkhah(tu)	(33) But when there comes the Deafening Blast	فَإِذَا جَآءَتِ ٱلصَّآخَّةُ ٣٣
Yawma Yafirru Al-Mar'u Min 'Akhīhi	(34) On the Day a man will flee from his brother	يَوۡمَ يَفِرُّ ٱلۡمَرۡءُ مِنۡ أَخِيهِ ٣٤
Wa 'Ummihi Wa 'Abīhi	(35) And his mother and his father	وَأُمِّهِۦ وَأَبِيهِ ٣٥
Wa Şāĥibatihi Wa Banīhi	(36) And his wife and his children,	وَصَٰحِبَتِهِۦ وَبَنِيهِ ٣٦
Likulli Amri'in Minhum Yawma'idhin Sha'nun Yughnīhi	(37) For every man, that Day, will be a matter adequate for him.	لِكُلِّ ٱمۡرِيٕٖ مِّنۡهُمۡ يَوۡمَئِذٖ شَأۡنٞ يُغۡنِيهِ ٣٧
Wujūhun Yawma'idhin Musfirah(tun)	(38) [Some] faces, that Day, will be bright -	وُجُوهٞ يَوۡمَئِذٖ مُّسۡفِرَةٞ ٣٨

Đaĥikatun Mustabshirah(tun)	(39) Laughing, rejoicing at good news.	ضَاحِكَةٌ مُّسْتَبْشِرَةٌ ﴿٣٩﴾
Wa Wujūhun Yawma'idhin `Alayhā Ghabarah(tun)	(40) And [other] faces, that Day, will have upon them dust.	وَوُجُوهٌ يَوْمَئِذٍ عَلَيْهَا غَبَرَةٌ ﴿٤٠﴾
Tarhaquhā Qatarah(tun)	(41) Blackness will cover them.	تَرْهَقُهَا قَتَرَةٌ ﴿٤١﴾
'Ūlā'ika Humu Al-Kafaratu Al-Fajarah(tu)	(42) Those are the disbelievers, the wicked ones.	أُوْلَـٰٓئِكَ هُمُ ٱلْكَفَرَةُ ٱلْفَجَرَةُ ﴿٤٢﴾

سورة التكوير

THE OVERTHROWING (81) At-Takwir

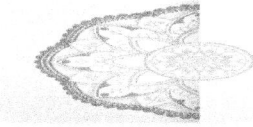

Bismi Al-Lahi Ar-Raĥmāni Ar-Raĥīmi	In the name of Allāh, the Entirely Merciful, the Especially Merciful.	بِسْمِ ٱللَّهِ ٱلرَّحْمَـٰنِ ٱلرَّحِيمِ
'Idhā Ash-Shamsu Kūwirat	(1) When the sun is wrapped up [in darkness]	إِذَا ٱلشَّمْسُ كُوِّرَتْ ﴿١﴾
Wa 'Idhā An-Nujūmu Ankadarat	(2) And when the stars fall, dispersing,	وَإِذَا ٱلنُّجُومُ ٱنكَدَرَتْ ﴿٢﴾
Wa 'Idhā Al-Jibālu Suyyirat	(3) And when the mountains are removed	وَإِذَا ٱلْجِبَالُ سُيِّرَتْ ﴿٣﴾

Wa 'Idhā Al-`Ishāru `Uţţilat	(4) And when full-term she-camels are neglected	وَإِذَا ٱلْعِشَارُ عُطِّلَتْ ٤
Wa 'Idhā Al-Wuĥūshu Ĥushirat	(5) And when the wild beasts are gathered	وَإِذَا ٱلْوُحُوشُ حُشِرَتْ ٥
Wa 'Idhā Al-Biĥāru Sujjirat	(6) And when the seas are filled with flame	وَإِذَا ٱلْبِحَارُ سُجِّرَتْ ٦
Wa 'Idhā An-Nufūsu Zūwijat	(7) And when the souls are paired	وَإِذَا ٱلنُّفُوسُ زُوِّجَتْ ٧
Wa 'Idhā Al-Maw'ūdatu Su'ilat	(8) And when the girl [who was] buried alive is asked	وَإِذَا ٱلْمَوْءُۥدَةُ سُئِلَتْ ٨
Bi'ayyi Dhanbin Qutilat	(9) For what sin she was killed	بِأَىِّ ذَنۢبٍ قُتِلَتْ ٩
Wa 'Idhā Aş-Şuĥufu Nushirat	(10) And when the pages are spread [i.e., made public]	وَإِذَا ٱلصُّحُفُ نُشِرَتْ ١٠
Wa 'Idhā As-Samā'u Kushiţat	(11) And when the sky is stripped away	وَإِذَا ٱلسَّمَآءُ كُشِطَتْ ١١
Wa 'Idhā Al-Jaĥīmu Su``irat	(12) And when Hellfire is set ablaze	وَإِذَا ٱلْجَحِيمُ سُعِّرَتْ ١٢
Wa 'Idhā Al-Jannatu 'Uzlifat	(13) And when Paradise is brought near,	وَإِذَا ٱلْجَنَّةُ أُزْلِفَتْ ١٣
`Alimat Nafsun Mā 'Aĥđarat	(14) A soul will [then] know what it has brought [with it].	عَلِمَتْ نَفْسٌ مَّآ أَحْضَرَتْ ١٤

Falā 'Uqsimu Bil-<u>Kh</u>unnasi	(15) So I swear by the retreating stars	فَلَآ أُقۡسِمُ بِٱلۡخُنَّسِ ١٥
Al-Jawāri Al-Kunnasi	(16) Those that run [their courses] and disappear [i.e., set]	ٱلۡجَوَارِ ٱلۡكُنَّسِ ١٦
Wa Al-Layli 'I<u>dh</u>ā \`As\`asa	(17) And by the night as it closes in	وَٱلَّيۡلِ إِذَا عَسۡعَسَ ١٧
Wa Aṣ-Ṣubĥi 'I<u>dh</u>ā Tanaffasa	(18) And by the dawn when it breathes [i.e., stirs]	وَٱلصُّبۡحِ إِذَا تَنَفَّسَ ١٨
'Innahu Laqawlu Rasūlin Karīmin	(19) [That] indeed, it [i.e., the Qur'ān] is a word [conveyed by] a noble messenger [i.e., Gabriel]	إِنَّهُۥ لَقَوۡلُ رَسُولٖ كَرِيمٖ ١٩
<u>Dh</u>ī Qūwatin \`Inda <u>Dh</u>ī Al-\`Ar<u>sh</u>i Makīnin	(20) [Who is] possessed of power and with the Owner of the Throne, secure [in position],	ذِي قُوَّةٍ عِندَ ذِي ٱلۡعَرۡشِ مَكِينٖ ٢٠
Muṭā\`in <u>Th</u>amma 'Amīnin	(21) Obeyed there [in the heavens] and trustworthy.	مُّطَاعٖ ثَمَّ أَمِينٖ ٢١
Wa Mā Ṣāĥibukum Bimajnūnin	(22) And your companion [i.e., Prophet Muḥammad (ﷺ)] is not [at all] mad.	وَمَا صَاحِبُكُم بِمَجۡنُونٖ ٢٢

Wa Laqad Ra'āhu Bil-'Ufuqi Al-Mubīni	(23) And he has already seen him [i.e., Gabriel] in the clear horizon.	وَلَقَدْ رَءَاهُ بِٱلْأُفُقِ ٱلْمُبِينِ ﴿٢٣﴾
Wa Mā Huwa `Alá Al-Ghaybi Biđanīnin	(24) And he [i.e., Muḥammad (ﷺ)] is not a withholder of [knowledge of] the unseen.	وَمَا هُوَ عَلَى ٱلْغَيْبِ بِضَنِينٍ ﴿٢٤﴾
Wa Mā Huwa Biqawli Shayţānin Rajīmin	(25) And it [i.e., the Qur'ān] is not the word of a devil, expelled [from the heavens].	وَمَا هُوَ بِقَوْلِ شَيْطَٰنٍ رَّجِيمٍ ﴿٢٥﴾
Fa'ayna Tadh/habūna	(26) So where are you going?	فَأَيْنَ تَذْهَبُونَ ﴿٢٦﴾
'In Huwa 'Illā Dhikrun Lil`ālamīna	(27) It is not except a reminder to the worlds	إِنْ هُوَ إِلَّا ذِكْرٌ لِّلْعَٰلَمِينَ ﴿٢٧﴾
Liman Shā'a Minkum 'An Yastaqīma	(28) For whoever wills among you to take a right course.	لِمَن شَآءَ مِنكُمْ أَن يَسْتَقِيمَ ﴿٢٨﴾
Wa Mā Tashā'ūna 'Illā 'An Yashā'a Al-Lahu Rabbu Al-`Ālamīna	(29) And you do not will except that Allāh wills - Lord of the worlds.	وَمَا تَشَآءُونَ إِلَّآ أَن يَشَآءَ ٱللَّهُ رَبُّ ٱلْعَٰلَمِينَ ﴿٢٩﴾

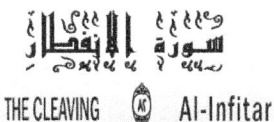

Bismi Al-Lahi Ar-Raĥmāni Ar-Raĥīmi	In the name of Allāh, the Entirely Merciful, the Especially Merciful.	بِسۡمِ ٱللَّهِ ٱلرَّحۡمَٰنِ ٱلرَّحِيمِ
'Idhā As-Samā'u Anfaţarat	(1) When the sky breaks apart	إِذَا ٱلسَّمَآءُ ٱنفَطَرَتۡ ١
Wa 'Idhā Al-Kawākibu Antatharat	(2) And when the stars fall, scattering,	وَإِذَا ٱلۡكَوَاكِبُ ٱنتَثَرَتۡ ٢
Wa 'Idhā Al-Biĥāru Fujjirat	(3) And when the seas are erupted	وَإِذَا ٱلۡبِحَارُ فُجِّرَتۡ ٣
Wa 'Idhā Al-Qubūru Bu`thirat	(4) And when the [contents of] graves are scattered [i.e., exposed],	وَإِذَا ٱلۡقُبُورُ بُعۡثِرَتۡ ٤
`Alimat Nafsun Mā Qaddamat Wa 'Akhkharat	(5) A soul will [then] know what it has put forth and kept back.	عَلِمَتۡ نَفۡسٞ مَّا قَدَّمَتۡ وَأَخَّرَتۡ ٥
Yā 'Ayyuhā Al-'Insānu Mā Gharraka Birabbika Al-Karīmi	(6) O mankind, what has deceived you concerning your Lord, the Generous,	يَٰٓأَيُّهَا ٱلۡإِنسَٰنُ مَا غَرَّكَ بِرَبِّكَ ٱلۡكَرِيمِ ٦

Al-Ladhī Khalaqaka Fasawwāka Fa`adalaka	(7) Who created you, proportioned you, and balanced you?	ٱلَّذِى خَلَقَكَ فَسَوَّىٰكَ فَعَدَلَكَ ٧
Fī 'Ayyi Şūratin Mā Shā'a Rakkabaka	(8) In whatever form He willed has He assembled you.	فِىٓ أَىِّ صُورَةٍ مَّا شَآءَ رَكَّبَكَ ٨
Kallā Bal Tukadhdhibūna Bid-Dīni	(9) No! But you deny the Recompense.	كَلَّا بَلْ تُكَذِّبُونَ بِٱلدِّينِ ٩
Wa 'Inna `Alaykum Laĥāfižīna	(10) And indeed, [appointed] over you are keepers,	وَإِنَّ عَلَيْكُمْ لَحَـٰفِظِينَ ١٠
Kirāmāan Kātibīna	(11) Noble and recording;	كِرَامًا كَـٰتِبِينَ ١١
Ya`lamūna Mā Taf`alūna	(12) They know whatever you do.	يَعْلَمُونَ مَا تَفْعَلُونَ ١٢
'Inna Al-'Abrāra Lafī Na`īmin	(13) Indeed, the righteous will be in pleasure,	إِنَّ ٱلْأَبْرَارَ لَفِى نَعِيمٍ ١٣
Wa 'Inna Al-Fujjāra Lafī Jaĥīmin	(14) And indeed, the wicked will be in Hellfire.	وَإِنَّ ٱلْفُجَّارَ لَفِى جَحِيمٍ ١٤
Yaşlawnahā Yawma Ad-Dīni	(15) They will [enter to] burn therein on the Day of Recompense,	يَصْلَوْنَهَا يَوْمَ ٱلدِّينِ ١٥

Wa Mā Hum `Anhā Bighā'ibīna	(16) And never therefrom will they be absent.	وَمَا هُمۡ عَنۡهَا بِغَآئِبِينَ ١٦
Wa Mā 'Adrāka Mā Yawmu Ad-Dīni	(17) And what can make you know what is the Day of Recompense?	وَمَآ أَدۡرَىٰكَ مَا يَوۡمُ ٱلدِّينِ ١٧
Thumma Mā 'Adrāka Mā Yawmu Ad-Dīni	(18) Then, what can make you know what is the Day of Recompense?	ثُمَّ مَآ أَدۡرَىٰكَ مَا يَوۡمُ ٱلدِّينِ ١٨
Yawma Lā Tamliku Nafsun Linafsin Shay'āan Wa Al-'Amru Yawma'idhin Lillahi	(19) It is the Day when a soul will not possess for another soul [power to do] a thing; and the command, that Day, is [entirely] with Allāh.	يَوۡمَ لَا تَمۡلِكُ نَفۡسٞ لِّنَفۡسٖ شَيۡـٔٗاۖ وَٱلۡأَمۡرُ يَوۡمَئِذٖ لِّلَّهِ ١٩

سورة المطففين

THE DEFRAUDING ٨٣ Al-Mutaffifin

Bismi Al-Lahi Ar-Raĥmāni Ar-Raĥīmi	In the name of Allāh, the Entirely Merciful, the Especially Merciful.	بِسۡمِ ٱللَّهِ ٱلرَّحۡمَٰنِ ٱلرَّحِيمِ
Waylun Lilmuţaffifīna	(1) Woe to those who give less [than due],	وَيۡلٞ لِّلۡمُطَفِّفِينَ ١

Al-Ladhīna 'Idhā Aktālū `Alá An-Nāsi Yastawfūna	(2) Who, when they take a measure from people, take in full.	ٱلَّذِينَ إِذَا ٱكْتَالُوا۟ عَلَى ٱلنَّاسِ يَسْتَوْفُونَ ٢
Wa 'Idhā Kālūhum 'Aw Wazanūhum Yukhsirūna	(3) But if they give by measure or by weight to them, they cause loss.	وَإِذَا كَالُوهُمْ أَو وَّزَنُوهُمْ يُخْسِرُونَ ٣
'Alā Yažunnu 'Ūla'ika 'Annahum Mab`ūthūna	(4) Do they not think that they will be resurrected	أَلَا يَظُنُّ أُو۟لَٰٓئِكَ أَنَّهُم مَّبْعُوثُونَ ٤
Liyawmin `Ažīmin	(5) For a tremendous Day -	لِيَوْمٍ عَظِيمٍ ٥
Yawma Yaqūmu An-Nāsu Lirabbi Al-`Ālamīna	(6) The Day when mankind will stand before the Lord of the worlds?	يَوْمَ يَقُومُ ٱلنَّاسُ لِرَبِّ ٱلْعَٰلَمِينَ ٦
Kallā 'Inna Kitāba Al-Fujjāri Lafī Sijjīnin	(7) No! Indeed, the record of the wicked is in sijjeen.	كَلَّآ إِنَّ كِتَٰبَ ٱلْفُجَّارِ لَفِى سِجِّينٍ ٧
Wa Mā 'Adrāka Mā Sijjīnun	(8) And what can make you know what is sijjeen?	وَمَآ أَدْرَىٰكَ مَا سِجِّينٌ ٨
Kitābun Marqūmun	(9) It is [their destination recorded in] a register inscribed.	كِتَٰبٌ مَّرْقُومٌ ٩
Waylun Yawma'idhin Lilmukadhdhibīna	(10) Woe, that Day, to the deniers,	وَيْلٌ يَوْمَئِذٍ لِّلْمُكَذِّبِينَ ١٠

Al-Ladhīna Yukadhdhibūna Biyawmi Ad-Dīni	(11) Who deny the Day of Recompense.	ٱلَّذِينَ يُكَذِّبُونَ بِيَوْمِ ٱلدِّينِ ﴿١١﴾
Wa Mā Yukadhdhibu Bihi 'Illā Kullu Mu`tadin 'Athīmin	(12) And none deny it except every sinful transgressor.	وَمَا يُكَذِّبُ بِهِۦٓ إِلَّا كُلُّ مُعْتَدٍ أَثِيمٍ ﴿١٢﴾
'Idhā Tutlá `Alayhi 'Āyātunā Qāla 'Asāţīru Al-'Awwalīna	(13) When Our verses are recited to him, he says, "Legends of the former peoples."	إِذَا تُتْلَىٰ عَلَيْهِ ءَايَٰتُنَا قَالَ أَسَٰطِيرُ ٱلْأَوَّلِينَ ﴿١٣﴾
Kallā Bal Rāna `Alá Qulūbihim Mā Kānū Yaksibūna	(14) No! Rather, the stain has covered their hearts of that which they were earning.	كَلَّا ۖ بَلْ ۜ رَانَ عَلَىٰ قُلُوبِهِم مَّا كَانُوا۟ يَكْسِبُونَ ﴿١٤﴾
Kallā 'Innahum `An Rabbihim Yawma'idhin Lamaĥjūbūna	(15) No! Indeed, from their Lord, that Day, they will be partitioned.	كَلَّآ إِنَّهُمْ عَن رَّبِّهِمْ يَوْمَئِذٍ لَّمَحْجُوبُونَ ﴿١٥﴾
Thumma 'Innahum Laşālū Al-Jaĥīmi	(16) Then indeed, they will [enter and] burn in Hellfire.	ثُمَّ إِنَّهُمْ لَصَالُوا۟ ٱلْجَحِيمِ ﴿١٦﴾
Thumma Yuqālu Hādhā Al-Ladhī Kuntum Bihi Tukadhdhibūna	(17) Then it will be said [to them], "This is what you used to deny."	ثُمَّ يُقَالُ هَٰذَا ٱلَّذِى كُنتُم بِهِۦ تُكَذِّبُونَ ﴿١٧﴾

Kallā 'Inna Kitāba Al-'Abrāri Lafī `Illīyīna	(18) No! Indeed, the record of the righteous is in ʿilliyyūn.	كَلَّآ إِنَّ كِتَـٰبَ ٱلْأَبْرَارِ لَفِى عِلِّيِّينَ ١٨
Wa Mā 'Adrāka Mā `Illīyūna	(19) And what can make you know what is ʿilliyyūn?	وَمَآ أَدْرَىٰكَ مَا عِلِّيُّونَ ١٩
Kitābun Marqūmun	(20) It is [their destination recorded in] a register inscribed	كِتَـٰبٌ مَّرْقُومٌ ٢٠
Yash/haduhu Al-Muqarrabūna	(21) Which is witnessed by those brought near [to Allāh].	يَشْهَدُهُ ٱلْمُقَرَّبُونَ ٢١
'Inna Al-'Abrāra Lafī Na`īmin	(22) Indeed, the righteous will be in pleasure	إِنَّ ٱلْأَبْرَارَ لَفِى نَعِيمٍ ٢٢
`Alá Al-'Arā'iki Yanžurūna	(23) On adorned couches, observing.	عَلَى ٱلْأَرَآئِكِ يَنظُرُونَ ٢٣
Ta`rifu Fī Wujūhihim Nađrata An-Na`īmi	(24) You will recognize in their faces the radiance of pleasure.	تَعْرِفُ فِى وُجُوهِهِمْ نَضْرَةَ ٱلنَّعِيمِ ٢٤
Yusqawna Min Raĥīqin Makhtūmin	(25) They will be given to drink [pure] wine [which was] sealed.	يُسْقَوْنَ مِن رَّحِيقٍ مَّخْتُومٍ ٢٥
Khitāmuhu Miskun Wa Fī Dhālika Falyatanāfasi Al-Mutanāfisūna	(26) The last of it is musk. So for this let the competitors compete.	خِتَـٰمُهُۥ مِسْكٌ وَفِى ذَٰلِكَ فَلْيَتَنَافَسِ ٱلْمُتَنَـٰفِسُونَ ٢٦

Wa Mizājuhu Min Tasnīmin	(27) And its mixture is of Tasneem,	وَمِزَاجُهُۥ مِن تَسْنِيمٍ ٢٧
`Aynāan Yashrabu Bihā Al-Muqarrabūna	(28) A spring from which those near [to Allāh] drink.	عَيْنًا يَشْرَبُ بِهَا ٱلْمُقَرَّبُونَ ٢٨
'Inna Al-Ladhīna 'Ajramū Kānū Mina Al-Ladhīna 'Āmanū Yađĥakūna	(29) Indeed, those who committed crimes used to laugh at those who believed.	إِنَّ ٱلَّذِينَ أَجْرَمُوا۟ كَانُوا۟ مِنَ ٱلَّذِينَ ءَامَنُوا۟ يَضْحَكُونَ ٢٩
Wa 'Idhā Marrū Bihim Yataghāmazūna	(30) And when they passed by them, they would exchange derisive glances.	وَإِذَا مَرُّوا۟ بِهِمْ يَتَغَامَزُونَ ٣٠
Wa 'Idhā Anqalabū 'Ilá 'Ahlihimu Anqalabū Fakihīna	(31) And when they returned to their people, they would return jesting.	وَإِذَا ٱنقَلَبُوٓا۟ إِلَىٰٓ أَهْلِهِمُ ٱنقَلَبُوا۟ فَكِهِينَ ٣١
Wa 'Idhā Ra'awhum Qālū 'Inna Hā'uulā' Lađāllūna	(32) And when they saw them, they would say, "Indeed, those are truly lost."	وَإِذَا رَأَوْهُمْ قَالُوٓا۟ إِنَّ هَٰٓؤُلَآءِ لَضَآلُّونَ ٣٢
Wa Mā 'Ursilū `Alayhim Ĥāfižīna	(33) But they had not been sent as guardians over them.	وَمَآ أُرْسِلُوا۟ عَلَيْهِمْ حَٰفِظِينَ ٣٣

Fālyawma Al-Ladhīna 'Āmanū Mina Al-Kuffāri Yađĥakūna	(34) So Today those who believed are laughing at the disbelievers,	فَٱلۡيَوۡمَ ٱلَّذِينَ ءَامَنُواْ مِنَ ٱلۡكُفَّارِ يَضۡحَكُونَ ٣٤
`Alá Al-'Arā'iki Yanžurūna	(35) On adorned couches, observing.	عَلَى ٱلۡأَرَآئِكِ يَنظُرُونَ ٣٥
Hal Thūwiba Al-Kuffāru Mā Kānū Yaf`alūna	(36) Have the disbelievers [not] been rewarded [this Day] for what they used to do?	هَلۡ ثُوِّبَ ٱلۡكُفَّارُ مَا كَانُواْ يَفۡعَلُونَ ٣٦

سورة الإنشقاق

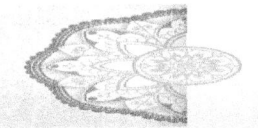

THE SUNDERING (84) Al-Inshiqaq

Bismi Al-Lahi Ar-Raĥmāni Ar-Raĥīmi	In the name of Allāh, the Entirely Merciful, the Especially Merciful.	بِسۡمِ ٱللَّهِ ٱلرَّحۡمَٰنِ ٱلرَّحِيمِ
'Idhā As-Samā'u Anshaqqat	(1) When the sky has split [open]	إِذَا ٱلسَّمَآءُ ٱنشَقَّتۡ ١
Wa 'Adhinat Lirabbihā Wa Ĥuqqat	(2) And has listened [i.e., responded] to its Lord and was obligated [to do so]	وَأَذِنَتۡ لِرَبِّهَا وَحُقَّتۡ ٢
Wa 'Idhā Al-'Arđu Muddat	(3) And when the earth has been extended	وَإِذَا ٱلۡأَرۡضُ مُدَّتۡ ٣

Wa 'Alqat Mā Fīhā Wa Takhallat	(4) And has cast out that within it and relinquished [it].	وَأَلْقَتْ مَا فِيهَا وَتَخَلَّتْ ٤
Wa 'Adhinat Lirabbihā Wa Ĥuqqat	(5) And has listened [i.e., responded] to its Lord and was obligated [to do so]	وَأَذِنَتْ لِرَبِّهَا وَحُقَّتْ ٥
Yā 'Ayyuhā Al-'Insānu 'Innaka Kādiĥun 'Ilá Rabbika Kadĥāan Famulāqīhi	(6) O mankind, indeed you are laboring toward your Lord with [great] exertion and will meet it.	يَٰٓأَيُّهَا ٱلْإِنسَٰنُ إِنَّكَ كَادِحٌ إِلَىٰ رَبِّكَ كَدْحًا فَمُلَٰقِيهِ ٦
Fa'ammā Man 'Ūtiya Kitābahu Biyamīnihi	(7) Then as for he who is given his record in his right hand,	فَأَمَّا مَنْ أُوتِيَ كِتَٰبَهُۥ بِيَمِينِهِۦ ٧
Fasawfa Yuĥāsabu Ĥisābāan Yasīrāan	(8) He will be judged with an easy account	فَسَوْفَ يُحَاسَبُ حِسَابًا يَسِيرًا ٨
Wa Yanqalibu 'Ilá 'Ahlihi Masrūrāan	(9) And return to his people in happiness.	وَيَنقَلِبُ إِلَىٰٓ أَهْلِهِۦ مَسْرُورًا ٩
Wa 'Ammā Man 'Ūtiya Kitābahu Warā'a Žahrihi	(10) But as for he who is given his record behind his back,	وَأَمَّا مَنْ أُوتِيَ كِتَٰبَهُۥ وَرَآءَ ظَهْرِهِۦ ١٠
Fasawfa Yad`ū Thubūrāan	(11) He will cry out for destruction	فَسَوْفَ يَدْعُوا۟ ثُبُورًا ١١

Wa Yaşlá Sa`īrāan	(12) And [enter to] burn in a Blaze.	وَيَصۡلَىٰ سَعِيرًا ١٢
'Innahu Kāna Fī 'Ahlihi Masrūrāan	(13) Indeed, he had [once] been among his people in happiness;	إِنَّهُۥ كَانَ فِيٓ أَهۡلِهِۦ مَسۡرُورًا ١٣
'Innahu Žanna 'An Lan Yaĥūra	(14) Indeed, he had thought he would never return [to Allāh].	إِنَّهُۥ ظَنَّ أَن لَّن يَحُورَ ١٤
Balá 'Inna Rabbahu Kāna Bihi Başīrāan	(15) But yes! Indeed, his Lord was ever, of him, Seeing.	بَلَىٰٓۚ إِنَّ رَبَّهُۥ كَانَ بِهِۦ بَصِيرٗا ١٥
Falā 'Uqsimu Bish-Shafaqi	(16) So I swear by the twilight glow	فَلَآ أُقۡسِمُ بِٱلشَّفَقِ ١٦
Wa Al-Layli Wa Mā Wasaqa	(17) And [by] the night and what it envelops	وَٱلَّيۡلِ وَمَا وَسَقَ ١٧
Wa Al-Qamari 'Idhā Attasaqa	(18) And [by] the moon when it becomes full	وَٱلۡقَمَرِ إِذَا ٱتَّسَقَ ١٨
Latarkabunna Ţabaqāan `An Ţabaqin	(19) [That] you will surely embark upon [i.e., experience] state after state.	لَتَرۡكَبُنَّ طَبَقًا عَن طَبَقٖ ١٩
Famā Lahum Lā Yu'uminūna	(20) So what is [the matter] with them [that] they do not believe,	فَمَا لَهُمۡ لَا يُؤۡمِنُونَ ٢٠

Wa 'Idhā Quri'a `Alayhimu Al-Qur'ānu Lā Yasjudūna	(21) And when the Qur'ān is recited to them, they do not prostrate [to Allāh]?	وَإِذَا قُرِئَ عَلَيْهِمُ ٱلْقُرْءَانُ لَا يَسْجُدُونَ ۩ ٢١
Bali Al-Ladhīna Kafarū Yukadhdhibūna	(22) But those who have disbelieved deny,	بَلِ ٱلَّذِينَ كَفَرُوا۟ يُكَذِّبُونَ ٢٢
Wa Allāhu 'A`lamu Bimā Yū`ūna	(23) And Allāh is most knowing of what they keep within themselves.	وَٱللَّهُ أَعْلَمُ بِمَا يُوعُونَ ٢٣
Fabashshirhum Bi`adhābin 'Alīmin	(24) So give them tidings of a painful punishment,	فَبَشِّرْهُم بِعَذَابٍ أَلِيمٍ ٢٤
'Illā Al-Ladhīna 'Āmanū Wa `Amilū Aş-Şāliĥāti Lahum 'Ajrun Ghayru Mamnūnin	(25) Except for those who believe and do righteous deeds. For them is a reward uninterrupted.	إِلَّا ٱلَّذِينَ ءَامَنُوا۟ وَعَمِلُوا۟ ٱلصَّـٰلِحَـٰتِ لَهُمْ أَجْرٌ غَيْرُ مَمْنُونٍۭ ٢٥

سورة البروج

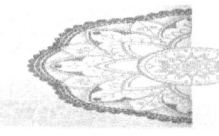

THE MANSIONS OF THE STARS (85) Al-Buruj

Bismi Al-Lahi Ar-Raĥmāni Ar-Raĥīmi	In the name of Allāh, the Entirely Merciful, the Especially Merciful.	بِسْمِ ٱللَّهِ ٱلرَّحْمَـٰنِ ٱلرَّحِيمِ
Wa As-Samā'i Dhāti Al-Burūji	(1) By the sky containing great stars	وَٱلسَّمَآءِ ذَاتِ ٱلْبُرُوجِ ١

Wa Al-Yawmi Al-Maw`ūdi	(2) And [by] the promised Day	وَٱلۡيَوۡمِ ٱلۡمَوۡعُودِ ٢
Wa Shāhidin Wa Mash/hūdin	(3) And [by] the witness and what is witnessed,	وَشَاهِدٖ وَمَشۡهُودٖ ٣
Qutila 'Aşĥābu Al-'Ukhdūdi	(4) Destroyed [i.e., cursed] were the companions of the trench	قُتِلَ أَصۡحَٰبُ ٱلۡأُخۡدُودِ ٤
An-Nāri Dhāti Al-Waqūdi	(5) [Containing] the fire full of fuel,	ٱلنَّارِ ذَاتِ ٱلۡوَقُودِ ٥
'Idh Hum `Alayhā Qu`ūdun	(6) When they were sitting near it.	إِذۡ هُمۡ عَلَيۡهَا قُعُودٞ ٦
Wa Hum `Alá Mā Yaf`alūna Bil-Mu'uminīna Shuhūdun	(7) And they, to what they were doing against the believers, were witnesses.	وَهُمۡ عَلَىٰ مَا يَفۡعَلُونَ بِٱلۡمُؤۡمِنِينَ شُهُودٞ ٧
Wa Mā Naqamū Minhum 'Illā 'An Yu'uminū Bil-Lahi Al-`Azīzi Al-Ĥamīdi	(8) And they resented them not except because they believed in Allāh, the Exalted in Might, the Praiseworthy,	وَمَا نَقَمُواْ مِنۡهُمۡ إِلَّآ أَن يُؤۡمِنُواْ بِٱللَّهِ ٱلۡعَزِيزِ ٱلۡحَمِيدِ ٨
Al-Ladhī Lahu Mulku As-Samāwāti Wa Al-'Arđi Wa Allāhu `Alá Kulli Shay'in Shahīdun	(9) To whom belongs the dominion of the heavens and the earth. And Allāh, over all things, is Witness.	ٱلَّذِي لَهُۥ مُلۡكُ ٱلسَّمَٰوَٰتِ وَٱلۡأَرۡضِۚ وَٱللَّهُ عَلَىٰ كُلِّ شَيۡءٖ شَهِيدٌ ٩

'Inna Al-Ladhīna Fatanū Al-Mu'uminīna Wa Al-Mu'umināti Thumma Lam Yatūbū Falahum `Adhābu Jahannama Wa Lahum `Adhābu Al-Ĥarīqi	(10) Indeed, those who have tortured the believing men and believing women and then have not repented will have the punishment of Hell, and they will have the punishment of the Burning Fire.	إِنَّ ٱلَّذِينَ فَتَنُوا۟ ٱلْمُؤْمِنِينَ وَٱلْمُؤْمِنَٰتِ ثُمَّ لَمْ يَتُوبُوا۟ فَلَهُمْ عَذَابُ جَهَنَّمَ وَلَهُمْ عَذَابُ ٱلْحَرِيقِ ١٠
'Inna Al-Ladhīna 'Āmanū Wa `Amilū Aş-Şāliĥāti Lahum Jannātun Tajrī Min Taĥtihā Al-'Anhāru Dhālika Al-Fawzu Al-Kabīru	(11) Indeed, those who have believed and done righteous deeds will have gardens beneath which rivers flow. That is the great attainment.	إِنَّ ٱلَّذِينَ ءَامَنُوا۟ وَعَمِلُوا۟ ٱلصَّٰلِحَٰتِ لَهُمْ جَنَّٰتٌ تَجْرِى مِن تَحْتِهَا ٱلْأَنْهَٰرُ ۚ ذَٰلِكَ ٱلْفَوْزُ ٱلْكَبِيرُ ١١
'Inna Baţsha Rabbika Lashadīdun	(12) Indeed, the assault [i.e., vengeance] of your Lord is severe.	إِنَّ بَطْشَ رَبِّكَ لَشَدِيدٌ ١٢
'Innahu Huwa Yubdi'u Wa Yu`īdu	(13) Indeed, it is He who originates [creation] and repeats.	إِنَّهُۥ هُوَ يُبْدِئُ وَيُعِيدُ ١٣

Wa Huwa Al-G̲h̲afūru Al-Wadūdu	(14) And He is the Forgiving, the Affectionate,	وَهُوَ ٱلْغَفُورُ ٱلْوَدُودُ ﴿١٤﴾
D̲h̲ū Al-`Ars̲h̲i Al-Majīdu	(15) Honorable Owner of the Throne,	ذُو ٱلْعَرْشِ ٱلْمَجِيدُ ﴿١٥﴾
Fa``ālun Limā Yurīdu	(16) Effecter of what He intends.	فَعَّالٌ لِّمَا يُرِيدُ ﴿١٦﴾
Hal 'Atāka Ĥadīt̲h̲u Al-Junūdi	(17) Has there reached you the story of the soldiers -	هَلْ أَتَىٰكَ حَدِيثُ ٱلْجُنُودِ ﴿١٧﴾
Fir`awna Wa T̲h̲amūda	(18) [Those of] Pharaoh and Thamūd?	فِرْعَوْنَ وَثَمُودَ ﴿١٨﴾
Bali Al-Lad̲h̲īna Kafarū Fī Takd̲h̲ībin	(19) But they who disbelieve are in [persistent] denial,	بَلِ ٱلَّذِينَ كَفَرُوا۟ فِى تَكْذِيبٍ ﴿١٩﴾
Wa Allāhu Min Warā'ihim Muĥīṭun	(20) While Allāh encompasses them from behind.	وَٱللَّهُ مِن وَرَآئِهِم مُّحِيطٌۢ ﴿٢٠﴾
Bal Huwa Qur'ānun Majīdun	(21) But this is an honored Qur'ān	بَلْ هُوَ قُرْءَانٌ مَّجِيدٌ ﴿٢١﴾
Fī Lawĥin Maĥfūẓin	(22) [Inscribed] in a Preserved Slate.	فِى لَوْحٍ مَّحْفُوظٍۭ ﴿٢٢﴾

Bismi Al-Lahi Ar-Rahmāni Ar-Rahīmi	In the name of Allāh, the Entirely Merciful, the Especially Merciful.	بِسۡمِ ٱللَّهِ ٱلرَّحۡمَٰنِ ٱلرَّحِيمِ
Wa As-Samā'i Wa Aţ-Ţāriqi	(1) By the sky and the night comer	وَٱلسَّمَآءِ وَٱلطَّارِقِ ١
Wa Mā 'Adrāka Mā Aţ-Ţāriqu	(2) And what can make you know what is the night comer?	وَمَآ أَدۡرَىٰكَ مَا ٱلطَّارِقُ ٢
An-Najmu Ath-Thāqibu	(3) It is the piercing star	ٱلنَّجۡمُ ٱلثَّاقِبُ ٣
'In Kullu Nafsin Lammā `Alayhā Ĥāfižun	(4) There is no soul but that it has over it a protector.	إِن كُلُّ نَفۡسٖ لَّمَّا عَلَيۡهَا حَافِظٞ ٤
Falyanžuri Al-'Insānu Mimma Khuliqa	(5) So let man observe from what he was created.	فَلۡيَنظُرِ ٱلۡإِنسَٰنُ مِمَّ خُلِقَ ٥
Khuliqa Min Mā'in Dāfiqin	(6) He was created from a fluid, ejected,	خُلِقَ مِن مَّآءٖ دَافِقٖ ٦
Yakhruju Min Bayni Aş-Şulbi Wa At-Tarā'ibi	(7) Emerging from between the backbone and the ribs.	يَخۡرُجُ مِنۢ بَيۡنِ ٱلصُّلۡبِ وَٱلتَّرَآئِبِ ٧

'Innahu `Alá Raj`ihi Laqādirun	(8) Indeed, He [i.e., Allāh], to return him [to life], is Able.	إِنَّهُۥ عَلَىٰ رَجۡعِهِۦ لَقَادِرٞ ٨
Yawma Tublá As-Sarā'iru	(9) The Day when secrets will be put on trial,	يَوۡمَ تُبۡلَى ٱلسَّرَآئِرُ ٩
Famā Lahu Min Qūwatin Wa Lā Nāşirin	(10) Then he [i.e., man] will have no power or any helper.	فَمَا لَهُۥ مِن قُوَّةٖ وَلَا نَاصِرٖ ١٠
Wa As-Samā'i Dhāti Ar-Raj`i	(11) By the sky which sends back	وَٱلسَّمَآءِ ذَاتِ ٱلرَّجۡعِ ١١
Wa Al-'Arđi Dhāti Aş-Şad`i	(12) And [by] the earth which splits,	وَٱلۡأَرۡضِ ذَاتِ ٱلصَّدۡعِ ١٢
'Innahu Laqawlun Faşlun	(13) Indeed, it [i.e., the Qur'ān] is a decisive statement,	إِنَّهُۥ لَقَوۡلٞ فَصۡلٞ ١٣
Wa Mā Huwa Bil-Hazli	(14) And it is not amusement.	وَمَا هُوَ بِٱلۡهَزۡلِ ١٤
'Innahum Yakīdūna Kaydāan	(15) Indeed, they are planning a plan,	إِنَّهُمۡ يَكِيدُونَ كَيۡدٗا ١٥
Wa 'Akīdu Kaydāan	(16) But I am planning a plan.	وَأَكِيدُ كَيۡدٗا ١٦
Famahhili Al-Kāfirīna 'Amhilhum Ruwaydāan	(17) So allow time for the disbelievers. Leave them awhile.	فَمَهِّلِ ٱلۡكَٰفِرِينَ أَمۡهِلۡهُمۡ رُوَيۡدَۢا ١٧

سورة الأعلى

THE MOST HIGH (87) Al-A'la

Bismi Al-Lahi Ar-Raĥmāni Ar-Raĥīmi	In the name of Allāh, the Entirely Merciful, the Especially Merciful.	بِسۡمِ ٱللَّهِ ٱلرَّحۡمَٰنِ ٱلرَّحِيمِ
Sabbiĥi Asma Rabbika Al-'A`lá	(1) Exalt the name of your Lord, the Most High,	سَبِّحِ ٱسۡمَ رَبِّكَ ٱلۡأَعۡلَى ١
Al-Ladhī Khalaqa Fasawwá	(2) Who created and proportioned	ٱلَّذِي خَلَقَ فَسَوَّىٰ ٢
Wa Al-Ladhī Qaddara Fahadá	(3) And who destined and [then] guided	وَٱلَّذِي قَدَّرَ فَهَدَىٰ ٣
Wa Al-Ladhī 'Akhraja Al-Mar`á	(4) And who brings out the pasture	وَٱلَّذِيٓ أَخۡرَجَ ٱلۡمَرۡعَىٰ ٤
Faja`alahu Ghuthā'an 'Aĥwá	(5) And [then] makes it black stubble.	فَجَعَلَهُۥ غُثَآءً أَحۡوَىٰ ٥
Sanuqri'uka Falā Tansá	(6) We will make you recite, [O Muḥammad], and you will not forget,	سَنُقۡرِئُكَ فَلَا تَنسَىٰٓ ٦

'Illā Mā Shā'a Al-Lahu 'Innahu Ya`lamu Al-Jahra Wa Mā Yakhfá	(7) Except what Allāh should will. Indeed, He knows what is declared and what is hidden.	إِلَّا مَا شَآءَ ٱللَّهُۚ إِنَّهُۥ يَعۡلَمُ ٱلۡجَهۡرَ وَمَا يَخۡفَىٰ ٧
Wa Nuyassiruka Lilyusrá	(8) And We will ease you toward ease.	وَنُيَسِّرُكَ لِلۡيُسۡرَىٰ ٨
Fadhakkir 'In Nafa`ati Adh-Dhikrá	(9) So remind, if the reminder should benefit;	فَذَكِّرۡ إِن نَّفَعَتِ ٱلذِّكۡرَىٰ ٩
Sayadhdhakkaru Man Yakhshá	(10) He who fears [Allāh] will be reminded.	سَيَذَّكَّرُ مَن يَخۡشَىٰ ١٠
Wa Yatajannabuhā Al-'Ashqá	(11) But the wretched one will avoid it	وَيَتَجَنَّبُهَا ٱلۡأَشۡقَى ١١
Al-Ladhī Yaşlá An-Nāra Al-Kubrá	(12) [He] who will [enter and] burn in the greatest Fire,	ٱلَّذِي يَصۡلَى ٱلنَّارَ ٱلۡكُبۡرَىٰ ١٢
Thumma Lā Yamūtu Fīhā Wa Lā Yaĥyā	(13) Neither dying therein nor living.	ثُمَّ لَا يَمُوتُ فِيهَا وَلَا يَحۡيَىٰ ١٣
Qad 'Aflaĥa Man Tazakká	(14) He has certainly succeeded who purifies himself	قَدۡ أَفۡلَحَ مَن تَزَكَّىٰ ١٤
Wa Dhakara Asma Rabbihi Faşallá	(15) And mentions the name of his Lord and prays.	وَذَكَرَ ٱسۡمَ رَبِّهِۦ فَصَلَّىٰ ١٥

Bal Tu'uthirūna Al-Ĥayāata Ad-Dunyā	(16) But you prefer the worldly life,	بَلْ تُؤْثِرُونَ ٱلْحَيَوٰةَ ٱلدُّنْيَا ١٦
Wa Al-'Ākhiratu Khayrun Wa 'Abqá	(17) While the Hereafter is better and more enduring.	وَٱلْـَٔاخِرَةُ خَيْرٌ وَأَبْقَىٰٓ ١٧
'Inna Hādhā Lafī Aş-Şuĥufi Al-'Ūlá	(18) Indeed, this is in the former scriptures,	إِنَّ هَٰذَا لَفِى ٱلصُّحُفِ ٱلْأُولَىٰ ١٨
Şuĥufi 'Ibrāhīma Wa Mūsá	(19) The scriptures of Abraham and Moses.	صُحُفِ إِبْرَٰهِيمَ وَمُوسَىٰ ١٩

سورة الغاشية

THE OVERWHELMING 88 Al-Ghashiyah

Bismi Al-Lahi Ar-Raĥmāni Ar-Raĥīmi	In the name of Allāh, the Entirely Merciful, the Especially Merciful.	بِسْمِ ٱللَّهِ ٱلرَّحْمَٰنِ ٱلرَّحِيمِ
Hal 'Atāka Ĥadīthu Al-Ghāshiyah(ti)	(1) Has there reached you the report of the Overwhelming [event]?	هَلْ أَتَىٰكَ حَدِيثُ ٱلْغَٰشِيَةِ ١
Wujūhun Yawma'idhin Khāshi`ah(tun)	(2) [Some] faces, that Day, will be humbled,	وُجُوهٌ يَوْمَئِذٍ خَٰشِعَةٌ ٢

`Āmilatun Nāşibah(tun)	(3) Working [hard] and exhausted.	عَامِلَةٌ نَّاصِبَةٌ ٣
Taşlá Nārāan Ĥāmiyah(tan)	(4) They will [enter to] burn in an intensely hot Fire.	تَصْلَىٰ نَارًا حَامِيَةً ٤
Tusqá Min `Aynin 'Āniyah(tin)	(5) They will be given drink from a boiling spring.	تُسْقَىٰ مِنْ عَيْنٍ ءَانِيَةٍ ٥
Laysa Lahum Ţa`āmun 'Illā Min Đarī`in	(6) For them there will be no food except from a poisonous, thorny plant	لَّيْسَ لَهُمْ طَعَامٌ إِلَّا مِن ضَرِيعٍ ٦
Lā Yusminu Wa Lā Yughnī Min Jū`in	(7) Which neither nourishes nor avails against hunger.	لَّا يُسْمِنُ وَلَا يُغْنِي مِن جُوعٍ ٧
Wujūhun Yawma'idhin Nā`imah(tun)	(8) [Other] faces, that Day, will show pleasure.	وُجُوهٌ يَوْمَئِذٍ نَّاعِمَةٌ ٨
Lisa`yihā Rāđiyah(tun)	(9) With their effort [they are] satisfied	لِّسَعْيِهَا رَاضِيَةٌ ٩
Fī Jannatin `Āliyah(tin)	(10) In an elevated garden,	فِي جَنَّةٍ عَالِيَةٍ ١٠
Lā Tasma`u Fīhā Lāghiyah(tan)	(11) Wherein they will hear no unsuitable speech.	لَّا تَسْمَعُ فِيهَا لَٰغِيَةً ١١
Fīhā `Aynun Jāriyah(tun)	(12) Within it is a flowing spring.	فِيهَا عَيْنٌ جَارِيَةٌ ١٢

Fīhā Sururun Marfū`ah(tun)	(13) Within it are couches raised high	فِيهَا سُرُرٌ مَّرۡفُوعَةٌ ١٣
Wa 'Akwābun Mawđū`ah(tun)	(14) And cups put in place	وَأَكۡوَابٌ مَّوۡضُوعَةٌ ١٤
Wa Namāriqu Maşfūfah(tun)	(15) And cushions lined up	وَنَمَارِقُ مَصۡفُوفَةٌ ١٥
Wa Zarābīyu Mabthūthah(tun)	(16) And carpets spread around.	وَزَرَابِيُّ مَبۡثُوثَةٌ ١٦
'Afalā Yanžurūna 'Ilá Al-'Ibili Kayfa Khuliqat	(17) Then do they not look at the camels - how they are created?	أَفَلَا يَنظُرُونَ إِلَى ٱلۡإِبِلِ كَيۡفَ خُلِقَتۡ ١٧
Wa 'Ilá As-Samā'i Kayfa Rufi`at	(18) And at the sky - how it is raised?	وَإِلَى ٱلسَّمَآءِ كَيۡفَ رُفِعَتۡ ١٨
Wa 'Ilá Al-Jibāli Kayfa Nuşibat	(19) And at the mountains - how they are erected?	وَإِلَى ٱلۡجِبَالِ كَيۡفَ نُصِبَتۡ ١٩
Wa 'Ilá Al-'Arđi Kayfa Suţiĥat	(20) And at the earth - how it is spread out?	وَإِلَى ٱلۡأَرۡضِ كَيۡفَ سُطِحَتۡ ٢٠
Fadhakkir 'Innamā 'Anta Mudhakkirun	(21) So remind, [O Muḥammad]; you are only a reminder.	فَذَكِّرۡ إِنَّمَآ أَنتَ مُذَكِّرٌ ٢١
Lasta `Alayhim Bimusayţirin	(22) You are not over them a controller.	لَّسۡتَ عَلَيۡهِم بِمُصَيۡطِرٍ ٢٢

'Illā Man Tawallá Wa Kafara	(23) However, he who turns away and disbelieves	إِلَّا مَن تَوَلَّىٰ وَكَفَرَ ﴿٢٣﴾
Fayu`adhdhibuhu Al-Lahu Al-`Adhāba Al-'Akbara	(24) Then Allāh will punish him with the greatest punishment.	فَيُعَذِّبُهُ ٱللَّهُ ٱلۡعَذَابَ ٱلۡأَكۡبَرَ ﴿٢٤﴾
'Inna 'Ilaynā 'Īābahum	(25) Indeed, to Us is their return.	إِنَّ إِلَيۡنَآ إِيَابَهُمۡ ﴿٢٥﴾
Thumma 'Inna `Alaynā Ĥisābahum	(26) Then indeed, upon Us is their account.	ثُمَّ إِنَّ عَلَيۡنَا حِسَابَهُم ﴿٢٦﴾

سورة الفجر

THE DAWN (89) Al-Fajr

Bismi Al-Lahi Ar-Raĥmāni Ar-Raĥīmi	In the name of Allāh, the Entirely Merciful, the Especially Merciful.	بِسۡمِ ٱللَّهِ ٱلرَّحۡمَٰنِ ٱلرَّحِيمِ
Wa Al-Fajri	(1) By the dawn	وَٱلۡفَجۡرِ ﴿١﴾
Wa Layālin `Ashrin	(2) And [by] ten nights	وَلَيَالٍ عَشۡرٖ ﴿٢﴾
Wa Ash-Shaf`i Wa Al-Watri	(3) And [by] the even [number] and the odd	وَٱلشَّفۡعِ وَٱلۡوَتۡرِ ﴿٣﴾
Wa Al-Layli 'Idhā Yasri	(4) And [by] the night when it passes,	وَٱلَّيۡلِ إِذَا يَسۡرِ ﴿٤﴾

Hal Fī Dhālika Qasamun Lidhī Ĥijrin	(5) Is there [not] in [all] that an oath [sufficient] for one of perception?	هَلْ فِى ذَٰلِكَ قَسَمٌ لِّذِى حِجْرٍ ٥
'Alam Tara Kayfa Fa`ala Rabbuka Bi`ādin	(6) Have you not considered how your Lord dealt with ʿAad -	أَلَمْ تَرَ كَيْفَ فَعَلَ رَبُّكَ بِعَادٍ ٦
'Irama Dhāti Al-`Imādi	(7) [With] Iram - who had lofty pillars,	إِرَمَ ذَاتِ ٱلْعِمَادِ ٧
Allatī Lam Yukhlaq Mithluhā Fī Al-Bilādi	(8) The likes of whom had never been created in the land?	ٱلَّتِى لَمْ يُخْلَقْ مِثْلُهَا فِى ٱلْبِلَٰدِ ٨
Wa Thamūda Al-Ladhīna Jābū Aş-Şakhra Bil-Wādi	(9) And [with] Thamūd, who carved out the rocks in the valley?	وَثَمُودَ ٱلَّذِينَ جَابُوا۟ ٱلصَّخْرَ بِٱلْوَادِ ٩
Wa Fir`awna Dhī Al-'Awtādi	(10) And [with] Pharaoh, owner of the stakes?	وَفِرْعَوْنَ ذِى ٱلْأَوْتَادِ ١٠
Al-Ladhīna Ţaghaw Fī Al-Bilādi	(11) [All of] whom oppressed within the lands	ٱلَّذِينَ طَغَوْا۟ فِى ٱلْبِلَٰدِ ١١
Fa'aktharū Fīhā Al-Fasāda	(12) And increased therein the corruption.	فَأَكْثَرُوا۟ فِيهَا ٱلْفَسَادَ ١٢
Faşabba `Alayhim Rabbuka Sawţa `Adhābin	(13) So your Lord poured upon them a scourge of punishment.	فَصَبَّ عَلَيْهِمْ رَبُّكَ سَوْطَ عَذَابٍ ١٣

'Inna Rabbaka Labiālmirşādi	(14) Indeed, your Lord is in observation.	إِنَّ رَبَّكَ لَبِٱلۡمِرۡصَادِ ١٤
Fa'ammā Al-'Insānu 'Idhā Mā Abtalāhu Rabbuhu Fa'akramahu Wa Na``amahu Fayaqūlu Rabbī 'Akramani	(15) And as for man, when his Lord tries him and [thus] is generous to him and favors him, he says, "My Lord has honored me."	فَأَمَّا ٱلۡإِنسَٰنُ إِذَا مَا ٱبۡتَلَىٰهُ رَبُّهُۥ فَأَكۡرَمَهُۥ وَنَعَّمَهُۥ فَيَقُولُ رَبِّيٓ أَكۡرَمَنِ ١٥
Wa 'Ammā 'Idhā Mā Abtalāhu Faqadara `Alayhi Rizqahu Fayaqūlu Rabbī 'Ahānani	(16) But when He tries him and restricts his provision, he says, "My Lord has humiliated me."	وَأَمَّآ إِذَا مَا ٱبۡتَلَىٰهُ فَقَدَرَ عَلَيۡهِ رِزۡقَهُۥ فَيَقُولُ رَبِّيٓ أَهَٰنَنِ ١٦
Kallā Bal Lā Tukrimūna Al-Yatīma	(17) No! But you do not honor the orphan	كَلَّاۖ بَل لَّا تُكۡرِمُونَ ٱلۡيَتِيمَ ١٧
Wa Lā Taĥāđđūna `Alá Ţa`āmi Al-Miskīni	(18) And you do not encourage one another to feed the poor.	وَلَا تَحَٰٓضُّونَ عَلَىٰ طَعَامِ ٱلۡمِسۡكِينِ ١٨
Wa Ta'kulūna At-Turātha 'Aklāan Lammāan	(19) And you consume inheritance, devouring [it] altogether,	وَتَأۡكُلُونَ ٱلتُّرَاثَ أَكۡلٗا لَّمّٗا ١٩
Wa Tuĥibbūna Al-Māla Ĥubbāan Jammāan	(20) And you love wealth with immense love.	وَتُحِبُّونَ ٱلۡمَالَ حُبّٗا جَمّٗا ٢٠

Kallā 'Idhā Dukkati Al-'Arđu Dakkāan Dakkāan	(21) No! When the earth has been leveled - pounded and crushed	كَلَّآ إِذَا دُكَّتِ ٱلۡأَرۡضُ دَكّٗا دَكّٗا ٢١
Wa Jā'a Rabbuka Wa Al-Malaku Şaffāan Şaffāan	(22) And your Lord has come and the angels, rank upon rank,	وَجَآءَ رَبُّكَ وَٱلۡمَلَكُ صَفّٗا صَفّٗا ٢٢
Wa Jī'a Yawma'idhin Bij ahannama Yawma'idhin Yatadhakkaru Al-'Insānu Wa 'Anná Lahu Adh-Dhikrá	(23) And brought [within view], that Day, is Hell - that Day, man will remember, but how [i.e., what good] to him will be the remembrance?	وَجِاْيٓءَ يَوۡمَئِذِۭ بِجَهَنَّمَۚ يَوۡمَئِذٖ يَتَذَكَّرُ ٱلۡإِنسَٰنُ وَأَنَّىٰ لَهُ ٱلذِّكۡرَىٰ ٢٣
Yaqūlu Yā Laytanī Qaddamtu Liĥayātī	(24) He will say, "Oh, I wish I had sent ahead [some good] for my life."	يَقُولُ يَٰلَيۡتَنِي قَدَّمۡتُ لِحَيَاتِي ٢٤
Fayawma'idhin Lā Yu`adhdhibu `Adhābahu 'Aĥadun	(25) So on that Day, none will punish [as severely] as His punishment,	فَيَوۡمَئِذٖ لَّا يُعَذِّبُ عَذَابَهُۥٓ أَحَدٞ ٢٥
Wa Lā Yūthiqu Wathāqahu 'Aĥadun	(26) And none will bind [as severely] as His binding [of the evildoers].	وَلَا يُوثِقُ وَثَاقَهُۥٓ أَحَدٞ ٢٦
Yā 'Ayyatuhā An-Nafsu Al-Muţma'innah(tu)	(27) [To the righteous it will be said], "O reassured soul,	يَٰٓأَيَّتُهَا ٱلنَّفۡسُ ٱلۡمُطۡمَئِنَّةُ ٢٧

Arji`ī 'Ilá Rabbiki Rāđiyatan Marđīyah(tan)	(28) Return to your Lord, well-pleased and pleasing [to Him],	ٱرْجِعِىٓ إِلَىٰ رَبِّكِ رَاضِيَةً مَّرْضِيَّةً ٢٨
Fādkhulī Fī `Ibādī	(29) And enter among My [righteous] servants	فَٱدْخُلِى فِى عِبَٰدِى ٢٩
Wa Adkhulī Jannatī	(30) And enter My Paradise."	وَٱدْخُلِى جَنَّتِى ٣٠

سورة البلد

THE CITY ٩٠ Al-Balad

Bismi Al-Lahi Ar-Raĥmāni Ar-Raĥīmi	In the name of Allāh, the Entirely Merciful, the Especially Merciful.	بِسْمِ ٱللَّهِ ٱلرَّحْمَٰنِ ٱلرَّحِيمِ
Lā 'Uqsimu Bihadhā Al-Baladi	(1) I swear by this city [i.e., Makkah]	لَآ أُقْسِمُ بِهَٰذَا ٱلْبَلَدِ ١
Wa 'Anta Ĥillun Bihadhā Al-Baladi	(2) And you, [O Muḥammad], are free of restriction in this city	وَأَنتَ حِلٌّۢ بِهَٰذَا ٱلْبَلَدِ ٢
Wa Wālidin Wa Mā Walada	(3) And [by] the father and that which was born [of him],	وَوَالِدٍ وَمَا وَلَدَ ٣
Laqad Khalaqnā Al-'Insāna Fī Kabadin	(4) We have certainly created man into hardship.	لَقَدْ خَلَقْنَا ٱلْإِنسَٰنَ فِى كَبَدٍ ٤

'Ayaĥsabu 'An Lan Yaqdira `Alayhi 'Aĥadun	(5) Does he think that never will anyone overcome him?	أَيَحۡسَبُ أَن لَّن يَقۡدِرَ عَلَيۡهِ أَحَدٞ ٥
Yaqūlu 'Ahlaktu Mālāan Lubadāan	(6) He says, "I have spent wealth in abundance."	يَقُولُ أَهۡلَكۡتُ مَالٗا لُّبَدًا ٦
'Ayaĥsabu 'An Lam Yarahu 'Aĥadun	(7) Does he think that no one has seen him?	أَيَحۡسَبُ أَن لَّمۡ يَرَهُۥٓ أَحَدٌ ٧
'Alam Naj`al Lahu `Aynayni	(8) Have We not made for him two eyes?	أَلَمۡ نَجۡعَل لَّهُۥ عَيۡنَيۡنِ ٨
Wa Lisānāan Wa Shafatayni	(9) And a tongue and two lips?	وَلِسَانٗا وَشَفَتَيۡنِ ٩
Wa Hadaynāhu An-Najdayni	(10) And have shown him the two ways?	وَهَدَيۡنَٰهُ ٱلنَّجۡدَيۡنِ ١٠
Falā Aqtaĥama Al-`Aqabah(ta)	(11) But he has not broken through the difficult pass.	فَلَا ٱقۡتَحَمَ ٱلۡعَقَبَةَ ١١
Wa Mā 'Adrāka Mā Al-`Aqabah(ta)	(12) And what can make you know what is [breaking through] the difficult pass?	وَمَآ أَدۡرَىٰكَ مَا ٱلۡعَقَبَةُ ١٢
Fakku Raqabah(tin)	(13) It is the freeing of a slave	فَكُّ رَقَبَةٍ ١٣

'Aw 'Iṭ`āmun Fī Yawmin Dhī Masghabah(tin)	(14) Or feeding on a day of severe hunger	أَوْ إِطْعَـٰمٌ فِى يَوْمٍ ذِى مَسْغَبَةٍ ﴿١٤﴾
Yatīmāan Dhā Maqrabah(tin)	(15) An orphan of near relationship	يَتِيمًا ذَا مَقْرَبَةٍ ﴿١٥﴾
'Aw Miskīnāan Dhā Matrabah(tin)	(16) Or a needy person in misery	أَوْ مِسْكِينًا ذَا مَتْرَبَةٍ ﴿١٦﴾
Thumma Kāna Mina Al-Ladhīna 'Āmanū Wa Tawāṣaw Biṣ-Ṣabri Wa Tawāṣaw Bil-Marĥamah(ti)	(17) And then being among those who believed and advised one another to patience and advised one another to compassion.	ثُمَّ كَانَ مِنَ ٱلَّذِينَ ءَامَنُواْ وَتَوَاصَوْاْ بِٱلصَّبْرِ وَتَوَاصَوْاْ بِٱلْمَرْحَمَةِ ﴿١٧﴾
'Ūlā'ika 'Aṣĥābu Al-Maymanah(ti)	(18) Those are the companions of the right.	أُوْلَـٰٓئِكَ أَصْحَـٰبُ ٱلْمَيْمَنَةِ ﴿١٨﴾
Wa Al-Ladhīna Kafarū Bi'āyātinā Hum 'Aṣĥābu Al-Mash'amah(ti)	(19) But they who disbelieved in Our signs - those are the companions of the left.	وَٱلَّذِينَ كَفَرُواْ بِـَٔايَـٰتِنَا هُمْ أَصْحَـٰبُ ٱلْمَشْـَٔمَةِ ﴿١٩﴾
`Alayhim Nārun Mu'uṣadah(tun)	(20) Over them will be fire closed in.	عَلَيْهِمْ نَارٌ مُّؤْصَدَةٌۢ ﴿٢٠﴾

Bismi Al-Lahi Ar-Raĥmāni Ar-Raĥīmi	In the name of Allāh, the Entirely Merciful, the Especially Merciful.	بِسۡمِ ٱللَّهِ ٱلرَّحۡمَٰنِ ٱلرَّحِيمِ
Wa Ash-Shamsi Wa Đuĥāhā	(1) By the sun and its brightness	وَٱلشَّمۡسِ وَضُحَىٰهَا ١
Wa Al-Qamari 'Idhā Talāhā	(2) And [by] the moon when it follows it	وَٱلۡقَمَرِ إِذَا تَلَىٰهَا ٢
Wa An-Nahāri 'Idhā Jallāhā	(3) And [by] the day when it displays it	وَٱلنَّهَارِ إِذَا جَلَّىٰهَا ٣
Wa Al-Layli 'Idhā Yaghshāhā	(4) And [by] the night when it covers [i.e., conceals] it	وَٱلَّيۡلِ إِذَا يَغۡشَىٰهَا ٤
Wa As-Samā'i Wa Mā Banāhā	(5) And [by] the sky and He who constructed it	وَٱلسَّمَآءِ وَمَا بَنَىٰهَا ٥
Wa Al-'Arđi Wa Mā Ṭaĥāhā	(6) And [by] the earth and He who spread it	وَٱلۡأَرۡضِ وَمَا طَحَىٰهَا ٦
Wa Nafsin Wa Mā Sawwāhā	(7) And [by] the soul and He who proportioned it	وَنَفۡسٖ وَمَا سَوَّىٰهَا ٧
Fa'alhamahā Fujūrahā Wa Taqwāhā	(8) And inspired it [with discernment of] its wickedness and its righteousness,	فَأَلۡهَمَهَا فُجُورَهَا وَتَقۡوَىٰهَا ٨

Qad 'Aflaĥa Man Zakkāhā	(9) He has succeeded who purifies it,	قَدْ أَفْلَحَ مَن زَكَّىٰهَا ٩
Wa Qad Khāba Man Dassāhā	(10) And he has failed who instills it [with corruption].	وَقَدْ خَابَ مَن دَسَّىٰهَا ١٠
Kadhdhabat Thamūdu Biţaghwāhā	(11) Thamūd denied [their prophet] by reason of their transgression,	كَذَّبَتْ ثَمُودُ بِطَغْوَىٰهَآ ١١
'Idhi Anba`atha 'Ashqāhā	(12) When the most wretched of them was sent forth.	إِذِ ٱنۢبَعَثَ أَشْقَىٰهَا ١٢
Faqāla Lahum Rasūlu Al-Lahi Nāqata Al-Lahi Wa Suqyāhā	(13) And the messenger of Allāh [i.e., Şāliḥ] said to them, "[Do not harm] the she-camel of Allāh or [prevent her from] her drink."	فَقَالَ لَهُمْ رَسُولُ ٱللَّهِ نَاقَةَ ٱللَّهِ وَسُقْيَٰهَا ١٣
Fakadhdhabūhu Fa`aqarūhā Fadamdama `Alayhim Rabbuhum Bidhanbihim Fasawwāhā	(14) But they denied him and hamstrung her. So their Lord brought down upon them destruction for their sin and made it equal [upon all of them].	فَكَذَّبُوهُ فَعَقَرُوهَا فَدَمْدَمَ عَلَيْهِمْ رَبُّهُم بِذَنۢبِهِمْ فَسَوَّىٰهَا ١٤
Wa Lā Yakhāfu `Uqbāhā	(15) And He does not fear the consequence thereof.	وَلَا يَخَافُ عُقْبَٰهَا ١٥

سورة الليل

THE NIGHT ٩٢ Al-Layl

Bismi Al-Lahi Ar-Raĥmāni Ar-Raĥīmi	In the name of Allāh, the Entirely Merciful, the Especially Merciful.	بِسۡمِ ٱللَّهِ ٱلرَّحۡمَٰنِ ٱلرَّحِيمِ
Wa Al-Layli 'Idhā Yaghshá	(1) By the night when it covers	وَٱلَّيۡلِ إِذَا يَغۡشَىٰ ١
Wa An-Nahāri 'Idhā Tajallá	(2) And [by] the day when it appears	وَٱلنَّهَارِ إِذَا تَجَلَّىٰ ٢
Wa Mā Khalaqa Adh-Dhakara Wa Al-'Unthá	(3) And [by] He who created the male and female,	وَمَا خَلَقَ ٱلذَّكَرَ وَٱلۡأُنثَىٰٓ ٣
'Inna Sa`yakum Lashattá	(4) Indeed, your efforts are diverse.	إِنَّ سَعۡيَكُمۡ لَشَتَّىٰ ٤
Fa'ammā Man 'A`ţá Wa Attaqá	(5) As for he who gives and fears Allāh	فَأَمَّا مَنۡ أَعۡطَىٰ وَٱتَّقَىٰ ٥
Wa Şaddaqa Bil-Ĥusná	(6) And believes in the best [reward],	وَصَدَّقَ بِٱلۡحُسۡنَىٰ ٦
Fasanuyassiruhu Lilyusrá	(7) We will ease him toward ease.	فَسَنُيَسِّرُهُۥ لِلۡيُسۡرَىٰ ٧
Wa 'Ammā Man Bakhila Wa Astaghná	(8) But as for he who withholds and considers himself free of need	وَأَمَّا مَنۢ بَخِلَ وَٱسۡتَغۡنَىٰ ٨

Wa Ka<u>dh</u><u>dh</u>aba Bil-Ḥusná	(9) And denies the best [reward],	۹ وَكَذَّبَ بِٱلْحُسْنَىٰ
Fasanuyassiruhu Lil`usrá	(10) We will ease him toward difficulty.	فَسَنُيَسِّرُهُۥ لِلْعُسْرَىٰ ۱۰
Wa Mā Yu<u>gh</u>nī `Anhu Māluhu 'I<u>dh</u>ā Taraddá	(11) And what will his wealth avail him when he falls?	وَمَا يُغْنِى عَنْهُ مَالُهُۥٓ إِذَا تَرَدَّىٰٓ ۱۱
'Inna `Alaynā Lalhudá	(12) Indeed, [incumbent] upon Us is guidance.	إِنَّ عَلَيْنَا لَلْهُدَىٰ ۱۲
Wa 'Inna Lanā Lal'ā<u>kh</u>irata Wa Al-'Ūlá	(13) And indeed, to us belongs the Hereafter and the first [life].	وَإِنَّ لَنَا لَلْءَاخِرَةَ وَٱلْأُولَىٰ ۱۳
Fa'an<u>dh</u>artukum Nārāan Talažžá	(14) So I have warned you of a Fire which is blazing.	فَأَنذَرْتُكُمْ نَارًا تَلَظَّىٰ ۱٤
Lā Yaşlāhā 'Illā Al-'A<u>sh</u>qá	(15) None will [enter to] burn therein except the most wretched one	لَا يَصْلَىٰهَآ إِلَّا ٱلْأَشْقَى ۱٥
Al-La<u>dh</u>ī Ka<u>dh</u><u>dh</u>aba Wa Tawallá	(16) Who had denied and turned away.	ٱلَّذِى كَذَّبَ وَتَوَلَّىٰ ۱٦
Wa Sayujannabuhā Al-'Atqá	(17) But the righteous one will avoid it	وَسَيُجَنَّبُهَا ٱلْأَتْقَى ۱۷
Al-La<u>dh</u>ī Yu'utī Mālahu Yatazakká	(18) [He] who gives [from] his wealth to purify himself	ٱلَّذِى يُؤْتِى مَالَهُۥ يَتَزَكَّىٰ ۱۸

Wa Mā Li'ĥadin `Indahu Min Ni`matin Tujzá	(19) And not [giving] for anyone who has [done him] a favor to be rewarded	وَمَا لِأَحَدٍ عِندَهُۥ مِن نِّعْمَةٍ تُجْزَىٰٓ ١٩
'Illā Abtighā'a Wajhi Rabbihi Al-'A`lá	(20) But only seeking the face [i.e., acceptance] of his Lord, Most High.	إِلَّا ٱبْتِغَآءَ وَجْهِ رَبِّهِ ٱلْأَعْلَىٰ ٢٠
Wa Lasawfa Yarđá	(21) And he is going to be satisfied.	وَلَسَوْفَ يَرْضَىٰ ٢١

سورة الضحى

THE MORNING HOURS ٩٣ Ad-Duhaa

Bismi Al-Lahi Ar-Raĥmāni Ar-Raĥīmi	In the name of Allāh, the Entirely Merciful, the Especially Merciful.	بِسْمِ ٱللَّهِ ٱلرَّحْمَٰنِ ٱلرَّحِيمِ
Wa Ađ-Đuĥá	(1) By the morning brightness	وَٱلضُّحَىٰ ١
Wa Al-Layli 'Idhā Sajá	(2) And [by] the night when it covers with darkness,	وَٱلَّيْلِ إِذَا سَجَىٰ ٢
Mā Wadda`aka Rabbuka Wa Mā Qalá	(3) Your Lord has not taken leave of you, [O Muḥammad], nor has He detested [you].	مَا وَدَّعَكَ رَبُّكَ وَمَا قَلَىٰ ٣
Wa Lal'ākhiratu Khayrun Laka Mina Al-'Ūlá	(4) And the Hereafter is better for you than the first [life].	وَلَلْءَاخِرَةُ خَيْرٌ لَّكَ مِنَ ٱلْأُولَىٰ ٤

Wa Lasawfa Yu`ţīka Rabbuka Fatarđá	(5) And your Lord is going to give you, and you will be satisfied.	وَلَسَوْفَ يُعْطِيكَ رَبُّكَ فَتَرْضَىٰٓ ٥
'Alam Yajidka Yatīmāan Fa'āwá	(6) Did He not find you an orphan and give [you] refuge?	أَلَمْ يَجِدْكَ يَتِيمًا فَـَٔاوَىٰ ٦
Wa Wajadaka Đāllāan Fahadá	(7) And He found you lost and guided [you],	وَوَجَدَكَ ضَآلًّا فَهَدَىٰ ٧
Wa Wajadaka `Ā'ilāan Fa'aghná	(8) And He found you poor and made [you] self-sufficient.	وَوَجَدَكَ عَآئِلًا فَأَغْنَىٰ ٨
Fa'ammā Al-Yatīma Falā Taqhar	(9) So as for the orphan, do not oppress [him].	فَأَمَّا ٱلْيَتِيمَ فَلَا تَقْهَرْ ٩
Wa 'Ammā As-Sā'ila Falā Tanhar	(10) And as for the petitioner, do not repel [him].	وَأَمَّا ٱلسَّآئِلَ فَلَا تَنْهَرْ ١٠
Wa 'Ammā Bini`mati Rabbika Fahaddith	(11) But as for the favor of your Lord, report [it].	وَأَمَّا بِنِعْمَةِ رَبِّكَ فَحَدِّثْ ١١

سورة الشرح

THE RELIEF 94 Ash-Sharh

Bismi Al-Lahi Ar-Rahmāni Ar-Rahīmi	In the name of Allāh, the Entirely Merciful, the Especially Merciful.	بِسْمِ ٱللَّهِ ٱلرَّحْمَٰنِ ٱلرَّحِيمِ

'Alam Nashraĥ Laka Şadraka	(1) Did We not expand for you, [O Muḥammad], your breast?	أَلَمْ نَشْرَحْ لَكَ صَدْرَكَ ١
Wa Wađa`nā `Anka Wizraka	(2) And We removed from you your burden	وَوَضَعْنَا عَنكَ وِزْرَكَ ٢
Al-Ladhī 'Anqađa Žahraka	(3) Which had weighed upon your back	ٱلَّذِىٓ أَنقَضَ ظَهْرَكَ ٣
Wa Rafa`nā Laka Dhikraka	(4) And raised high for you your repute.	وَرَفَعْنَا لَكَ ذِكْرَكَ ٤
Fa'inna Ma`a Al-`Usri Yusrāan	(5) For indeed, with hardship [will be] ease [i.e., relief].	فَإِنَّ مَعَ ٱلْعُسْرِ يُسْرًا ٥
'Inna Ma`a Al-`Usri Yusrāan	(6) Indeed, with hardship [will be] ease.	إِنَّ مَعَ ٱلْعُسْرِ يُسْرًا ٦
Fa'idhā Faraghta Fānşab	(7) So when you have finished [your duties], then stand up [for worship].	فَإِذَا فَرَغْتَ فَٱنصَبْ ٧
Wa 'Ilá Rabbika Fārghab	(8) And to your Lord direct [your] longing.	وَإِلَىٰ رَبِّكَ فَٱرْغَب ٨

سورة التين

THE FIG 95 At-Tin

Bismi Al-Lahi Ar-Raĥmāni Ar-Raĥīmi	In the name of Allāh, the Entirely Merciful, the Especially Merciful.	بِسۡمِ ٱللَّهِ ٱلرَّحۡمَٰنِ ٱلرَّحِيمِ
Wa At-Tīni Wa Az-Zaytūni	(1) By the fig and the olive	وَٱلتِّينِ وَٱلزَّيۡتُونِ ١
Wa Ṭūri Sīnīna	(2) And [by] Mount Sinai	وَطُورِ سِينِينَ ٢
Wa Hadhā Al-Baladi Al-'Amīni	(3) And [by] this secure city [i.e., Makkah],	وَهَٰذَا ٱلۡبَلَدِ ٱلۡأَمِينِ ٣
Laqad Khalaqnā Al-'Insāna Fī 'Aĥsani Taqwīmin	(4) We have certainly created man in the best of stature;	لَقَدۡ خَلَقۡنَا ٱلۡإِنسَٰنَ فِيٓ أَحۡسَنِ تَقۡوِيمٖ ٤
Thumma Radadnāhu 'Asfala Sāfilīna	(5) Then We return him to the lowest of the low,	ثُمَّ رَدَدۡنَٰهُ أَسۡفَلَ سَٰفِلِينَ ٥
'Illā Al-Ladhīna 'Āmanū Wa `Amilū Aṣ-Ṣāliĥāti Falahum 'Ajrun Ghayru Mamnūnin	(6) Except for those who believe and do righteous deeds, for they will have a reward uninterrupted.	إِلَّا ٱلَّذِينَ ءَامَنُواْ وَعَمِلُواْ ٱلصَّٰلِحَٰتِ فَلَهُمۡ أَجۡرٌ غَيۡرُ مَمۡنُونٖ ٦
Famā Yukadhdhibuka Ba`du Bid-Dīni	(7) So what yet causes you to deny the Recompense?	فَمَا يُكَذِّبُكَ بَعۡدُ بِٱلدِّينِ ٧
'Alaysa Al-Lahu Bi'aĥkami Al-Ĥākimīna	(8) Is not Allāh the most just of judges?	أَلَيۡسَ ٱللَّهُ بِأَحۡكَمِ ٱلۡحَٰكِمِينَ ٨

Bismi Al-Lahi Ar-Raĥmāni Ar-Raĥīmi	In the name of Allāh, the Entirely Merciful, the Especially Merciful.	بِسۡمِ ٱللَّهِ ٱلرَّحۡمَٰنِ ٱلرَّحِيمِ
Aqra' Biāsmi Rabbika Al-Ladhī Khalaqa	(1) Recite in the name of your Lord who created	ٱقۡرَأۡ بِٱسۡمِ رَبِّكَ ٱلَّذِى خَلَقَ ١
Khalaqa Al-'Insāna Min `Alaqin	(2) Created man from a clinging substance.	خَلَقَ ٱلۡإِنسَٰنَ مِنۡ عَلَقٍ ٢
Aqra' Wa Rabbuka Al-'Akramu	(3) Recite, and your Lord is the most Generous -	ٱقۡرَأۡ وَرَبُّكَ ٱلۡأَكۡرَمُ ٣
Al-Ladhī `Allama Bil-Qalami	(4) Who taught by the pen	ٱلَّذِى عَلَّمَ بِٱلۡقَلَمِ ٤
`Allama Al-'Insāna Mā Lam Ya`lam	(5) Taught man that which he knew not.	عَلَّمَ ٱلۡإِنسَٰنَ مَا لَمۡ يَعۡلَمۡ ٥
Kallā 'Inna Al-'Insāna Layaţghá	(6) No! [But] indeed, man transgresses	كَلَّآ إِنَّ ٱلۡإِنسَٰنَ لَيَطۡغَىٰٓ ٦
'An Ra'āhu Astaghná	(7) Because he sees himself self-sufficient.	أَن رَّءَاهُ ٱسۡتَغۡنَىٰٓ ٧

'Inna 'Ilá Rabbika Ar-Ruj`á	(8) Indeed, to your Lord is the return.	إِنَّ إِلَىٰ رَبِّكَ ٱلرُّجۡعَىٰٓ ٨
'Ara'ayta Al-Ladhī Yanhá	(9) Have you seen the one who forbids	أَرَءَيۡتَ ٱلَّذِي يَنۡهَىٰ ٩
`Abdāan 'Idhā Şallá	(10) A servant when he prays?	عَبۡدًا إِذَا صَلَّىٰٓ ١٠
'Ara'ayta 'In Kāna `Alá Al-Hudá	(11) Have you seen if he is upon guidance	أَرَءَيۡتَ إِن كَانَ عَلَى ٱلۡهُدَىٰٓ ١١
'Aw 'Amara Bit-Taqwá	(12) Or enjoins righteousness?	أَوۡ أَمَرَ بِٱلتَّقۡوَىٰٓ ١٢
'Ara'ayta 'In Kadhdhaba Wa Tawallá	(13) Have you seen if he denies and turns away -	أَرَءَيۡتَ إِن كَذَّبَ وَتَوَلَّىٰٓ ١٣
'Alam Ya`lam Bi'anna Al-Laha Yará	(14) Does he not know that Allāh sees?	أَلَمۡ يَعۡلَم بِأَنَّ ٱللَّهَ يَرَىٰ ١٤
Kallā La'in Lam Yantahi Lanasfa`ā Bin-Nāşiyah(ti)	(15) No! If he does not desist, We will surely drag him by the forelock	كَلَّا لَئِن لَّمۡ يَنتَهِ لَنَسۡفَعَۢا بِٱلنَّاصِيَةِ ١٥
Nāşiyatin Kādhibatin Khāţi'ah(tin)	(16) A lying, sinning forelock.	نَاصِيَةٖ كَٰذِبَةٍ خَاطِئَةٖ ١٦
Falyad`u Nādiyahu	(17) Then let him call his associates;	فَلۡيَدۡعُ نَادِيَهُۥ ١٧
Sanad`u Az-Zabāniyah(ta)	(18) We will call the angels of Hell.	سَنَدۡعُ ٱلزَّبَانِيَةَ ١٨

Kallā Lā Tuṭi`hu Wa Asjud Wāqtarib	(19) No! Do not obey him. But prostrate and draw near [to Allāh].	كَلَّا لَا تُطِعْهُ وَٱسْجُدْ وَٱقْتَرِب ۩ ١٩

سورة القدر

THE POWER (٩٧) Al-Qadr

Bismi Al-Lahi Ar-Raĥmāni Ar-Raĥīmi	In the name of Allāh, the Entirely Merciful, the Especially Merciful.	بِسْمِ ٱللَّهِ ٱلرَّحْمَٰنِ ٱلرَّحِيمِ
'Innā 'Anzalnāhu Fī Laylati Al-Qadri	(1) Indeed, We sent it [i.e., the Qur'ān] down during the Night of Decree.	إِنَّآ أَنزَلْنَٰهُ فِى لَيْلَةِ ٱلْقَدْرِ ١
Wa Mā 'Adrāka Mā Laylatu Al-Qadri	(2) And what can make you know what is the Night of Decree?	وَمَآ أَدْرَىٰكَ مَا لَيْلَةُ ٱلْقَدْرِ ٢
Laylatu Al-Qadri Khayrun Min 'Alfi Shahrin	(3) The Night of Decree is better than a thousand months.	لَيْلَةُ ٱلْقَدْرِ خَيْرٌ مِّنْ أَلْفِ شَهْرٍ ٣
Tanazzalu Al-Malā'ikatu Wa Ar-Rūĥu Fīhā Bi'idhni Rabbihim Min Kulli 'Amrin	(4) The angels and the Spirit [i.e., Gabriel] descend therein by permission of their Lord for every matter.	تَنَزَّلُ ٱلْمَلَٰٓئِكَةُ وَٱلرُّوحُ فِيهَا بِإِذْنِ رَبِّهِم مِّن كُلِّ أَمْرٍ ٤
Salāmun Hiya Ĥattá Maṭla`i Al-Fajri	(5) Peace it is until the emergence of dawn.	سَلَٰمٌ هِىَ حَتَّىٰ مَطْلَعِ ٱلْفَجْرِ ٥

سورة البينة

THE CLEAR PROOF ٩٨ Al-Bayyinah

Bismi Al-Lahi Ar-Raĥmāni Ar-Raĥīmi	In the name of Allāh, the Entirely Merciful, the Especially Merciful.	بِسۡمِ ٱللَّهِ ٱلرَّحۡمَٰنِ ٱلرَّحِيمِ
Lam Yakuni Al-Ladhīna Kafarū Min 'Ahli Al-Kitābi Wa Al-Mushrikīna Munfakkīna Ĥattá Ta'tiyahumu Al-Bayyinah(tu)	(1) Those who disbelieved among the People of the Scripture and the polytheists were not to be parted [from misbelief] until there came to them clear evidence	لَمۡ يَكُنِ ٱلَّذِينَ كَفَرُواْ مِنۡ أَهۡلِ ٱلۡكِتَٰبِ وَٱلۡمُشۡرِكِينَ مُنفَكِّينَ حَتَّىٰ تَأۡتِيَهُمُ ٱلۡبَيِّنَةُ ١
Rasūlun Mina Al-Lahi Yatlū Şuĥufāan Muţahharah(tan)	(2) A Messenger from Allāh, reciting purified scriptures	رَسُولٞ مِّنَ ٱللَّهِ يَتۡلُواْ صُحُفٗا مُّطَهَّرَةٗ ٢
Fīhā Kutubun Qayyimah(tun)	(3) Within which are correct writings [i.e., rulings and laws].	فِيهَا كُتُبٞ قَيِّمَةٞ ٣
Wa Mā Tafarraqa Al-Ladhīna 'Ūtū Al-Kitāba 'Illā Min Ba`di Mā Jā'at/humu Al-Bayyinah(tu)	(4) Nor did those who were given the Scripture become divided until after there had come to them clear evidence.	وَمَا تَفَرَّقَ ٱلَّذِينَ أُوتُواْ ٱلۡكِتَٰبَ إِلَّا مِنۢ بَعۡدِ مَا جَآءَتۡهُمُ ٱلۡبَيِّنَةُ ٤

Wa Mā 'Umirū 'Illā Liya`budū Al-Laha Mukhlişīna Lahu Ad-Dīna Ĥunafā'a Wa Yuqīmū Aş-Şalāata Wa Yu'utū Az-Zakāata Wa Dhalika Dīnu Al-Qayyimah(ti)	(5) And they were not commanded except to worship Allāh, [being] sincere to Him in religion, inclining to truth, and to establish prayer and to give zakāh. And that is the correct religion.	وَمَآ أُمِرُوٓا۟ إِلَّا لِيَعۡبُدُوا۟ ٱللَّهَ مُخۡلِصِينَ لَهُ ٱلدِّينَ حُنَفَآءَ وَيُقِيمُوا۟ ٱلصَّلَوٰةَ وَيُؤۡتُوا۟ ٱلزَّكَوٰةَۚ وَذَٰلِكَ دِينُ ٱلۡقَيِّمَةِ ٥
'Inna Al-Ladhīna Kafarū Min 'Ahli Al-Kitābi Wa Al-Mushrikīna Fī Nāri Jahannama Khālidīna Fīhā 'Ūlā'ika Hum Sharru Al-Barīyah(ti)	(6) Indeed, they who disbelieved among the People of the Scripture and the polytheists will be in the fire of Hell, abiding eternally therein. Those are the worst of creatures.	إِنَّ ٱلَّذِينَ كَفَرُوا۟ مِنۡ أَهۡلِ ٱلۡكِتَٰبِ وَٱلۡمُشۡرِكِينَ فِي نَارِ جَهَنَّمَ خَٰلِدِينَ فِيهَآۚ أُو۟لَٰٓئِكَ هُمۡ شَرُّ ٱلۡبَرِيَّةِ ٦
'Inna Al-Ladhīna 'Āmanū Wa `Amilū Aş-Şāliĥāti 'Ūlā'ika Hum Khayru Al-Barīyah(ti)	(7) Indeed, they who have believed and done righteous deeds - those are the best of creatures.	إِنَّ ٱلَّذِينَ ءَامَنُوا۟ وَعَمِلُوا۟ ٱلصَّٰلِحَٰتِ أُو۟لَٰٓئِكَ هُمۡ خَيۡرُ ٱلۡبَرِيَّةِ ٧

Jazā'uuhum `Inda Rabbihim Jannātu `Adnin Tajrī Min Taĥtihā Al-'Anhāru Khālidīna Fīhā 'Abadāan Rađiya Al-Lahu `Anhum Wa Rađū `Anhu Dhālika Liman Khashiya Rabbahu	(8) Their reward with their Lord will be gardens of perpetual residence beneath which rivers flow, wherein they will abide forever, Allāh being pleased with them and they with Him. That is for whoever has feared his Lord.	جَزَآؤُهُمۡ عِندَ رَبِّهِمۡ جَنَّٰتُ عَدۡنٖ تَجۡرِي مِن تَحۡتِهَا ٱلۡأَنۡهَٰرُ خَٰلِدِينَ فِيهَآ أَبَدٗاۖ رَّضِيَ ٱللَّهُ عَنۡهُمۡ وَرَضُواْ عَنۡهُۚ ذَٰلِكَ لِمَنۡ خَشِيَ رَبَّهُۥ ٨

سُورَةُ الزَّلْزَلَةِ

THE EARTHQUAKE (٩٩) Az-Zalzalah

Bismi Al-Lahi Ar-Raĥmāni Ar-Raĥīmi	In the name of Allāh, the Entirely Merciful, the Especially Merciful.	بِسۡمِ ٱللَّهِ ٱلرَّحۡمَٰنِ ٱلرَّحِيمِ
'Idhā Zulzilati Al-'Arđu Zilzālahā	(1) When the earth is shaken with its [final] earthquake	إِذَا زُلۡزِلَتِ ٱلۡأَرۡضُ زِلۡزَالَهَا ١
Wa 'Akhrajati Al-'Arđu 'Athqālahā	(2) And the earth discharges its burdens	وَأَخۡرَجَتِ ٱلۡأَرۡضُ أَثۡقَالَهَا ٢
Wa Qāla Al-'Insānu Mā Lahā	(3) And man says, "What is [wrong] with it?"	وَقَالَ ٱلۡإِنسَٰنُ مَا لَهَا ٣
Yawma'idhin Tuĥaddithu 'Akhbārahā	(4) That Day, it will report its news	يَوۡمَئِذٖ تُحَدِّثُ أَخۡبَارَهَا ٤

Bi'anna Rabbaka 'Awĥá Lahā	(5) Because your Lord has inspired [i.e., commanded] it.	بِأَنَّ رَبَّكَ أَوْحَىٰ لَهَا ٥
Yawma'idhin Yaşduru An-Nāsu 'Ashtātāan Liyuraw 'A`mālahum	(6) That Day, the people will depart separated [into categories] to be shown [the result of] their deeds.	يَوْمَئِذٍ يَصْدُرُ ٱلنَّاسُ أَشْتَاتًا لِّيُرَوْا۟ أَعْمَٰلَهُمْ ٦
Faman Ya`mal Mithqāla Dharratin Khayrāan Yarahu	(7) So whoever does an atom's weight of good will see it,	فَمَن يَعْمَلْ مِثْقَالَ ذَرَّةٍ خَيْرًا يَرَهُۥ ٧
Wa Man Ya`mal Mithqāla Dharratin Sharrāan Yarahu	(8) And whoever does an atom's weight of evil will see it.	وَمَن يَعْمَلْ مِثْقَالَ ذَرَّةٍ شَرًّا يَرَهُۥ ٨

سورة العاديات

THE COURSER 100 Al-'Adiyat

Bismi Al-Lahi Ar-Raĥmāni Ar-Raĥīmi	In the name of Allāh, the Entirely Merciful, the Especially Merciful.	بِسْمِ ٱللَّهِ ٱلرَّحْمَٰنِ ٱلرَّحِيمِ
Wa Al-`Ādiyāti Đabĥāan	(1) By the racers, panting,	وَٱلْعَٰدِيَٰتِ ضَبْحًا ١

Fālmūriyāti Qadĥāan	(2) And the producers of sparks [when] striking	فَٱلۡمُورِيَٰتِ قَدۡحٗا ٢
Fālmughīrāti Şubĥāan	(3) And the chargers at dawn,	فَٱلۡمُغِيرَٰتِ صُبۡحٗا ٣
Fa'atharna Bihi Naq`āan	(4) Stirring up thereby [clouds of] dust,	فَأَثَرۡنَ بِهِۦ نَقۡعٗا ٤
Fawasaţna Bihi Jam`āan	(5) Arriving thereby in the center collectively,	فَوَسَطۡنَ بِهِۦ جَمۡعًا ٥
'Inna Al-'Insāna Lirabbihi Lakanūdun	(6) Indeed mankind, to his Lord, is ungrateful.	إِنَّ ٱلۡإِنسَٰنَ لِرَبِّهِۦ لَكَنُودٞ ٦
Wa 'Innahu `Alá Dhālika Lashahīdun	(7) And indeed, he is to that a witness.	وَإِنَّهُۥ عَلَىٰ ذَٰلِكَ لَشَهِيدٞ ٧
Wa 'Innahu Liĥubbi Al-Khayri Lashadīdun	(8) And indeed he is, in love of wealth, intense.	وَإِنَّهُۥ لِحُبِّ ٱلۡخَيۡرِ لَشَدِيدٌ ٨
'Afalā Ya`lamu 'Idhā Bu`thira Mā Fī Al-Qubūri	(9) But does he not know that when the contents of the graves are scattered	۞أَفَلَا يَعۡلَمُ إِذَا بُعۡثِرَ مَا فِي ٱلۡقُبُورِ ٩
Wa Ĥuşşila Mā Fī Aş-Şudūri	(10) And that within the breasts is obtained,	وَحُصِّلَ مَا فِي ٱلصُّدُورِ ١٠
'Inna Rabbahum Bihim Yawma'idhin Lakhabīrun	(11) Indeed, their Lord with them, that Day, is [fully] Aware.	إِنَّ رَبَّهُم بِهِمۡ يَوۡمَئِذٖ لَّخَبِيرُۢ ١١

سُورَةُ القَارِعَة

THE CALAMITY (101) Al-Qari'ah

Bismi Al-Lahi Ar-Raĥmāni Ar-Raĥīmi	In the name of Allāh, the Entirely Merciful, the Especially Merciful.	بِسۡمِ ٱللَّهِ ٱلرَّحۡمَٰنِ ٱلرَّحِيمِ
Al-Qāri`ah(tu)	(1) The Striking Calamity	ٱلۡقَارِعَةُ ١
Mā Al-Qāri`ah(tu)	(2) What is the Striking Calamity?	مَا ٱلۡقَارِعَةُ ٢
Wa Mā 'Adrāka Mā Al-Qāri`ah(tu)	(3) And what can make you know what is the Striking Calamity?	وَمَآ أَدۡرَىٰكَ مَا ٱلۡقَارِعَةُ ٣
Yawma Yakūnu An-Nāsu Kālfarāshi Al-Mabthūthi	(4) It is the Day when people will be like moths, dispersed,	يَوۡمَ يَكُونُ ٱلنَّاسُ كَٱلۡفَرَاشِ ٱلۡمَبۡثُوثِ ٤
Wa Takūnu Al-Jibālu Kāl`ihni Al-Manfūshi	(5) And the mountains will be like wool, fluffed up.	وَتَكُونُ ٱلۡجِبَالُ كَٱلۡعِهۡنِ ٱلۡمَنفُوشِ ٥
Fa'ammā Man Thaqulat Mawāzīnuhu	(6) Then as for one whose scales are heavy [with good deeds],	فَأَمَّا مَن ثَقُلَتۡ مَوَٰزِينُهُۥ ٦

Fahuwa Fī `Īshatin Rāđiyah(tin)	(7) He will be in a pleasant life.	فَهُوَ فِي عِيشَةٖ رَّاضِيَةٖ ٧
Wa 'Ammā Man Khaffat Mawāzīnuhu	(8) But as for one whose scales are light,	وَأَمَّا مَنۡ خَفَّتۡ مَوَٰزِينُهُۥ ٨
Fa'ummuhu Hāwiyah(tun)	(9) His refuge will be an abyss.	فَأُمُّهُۥ هَاوِيَةٞ ٩
Wa Mā 'Adrāka Mā Hiyah	(10) And what can make you know what that is?	وَمَآ أَدۡرَىٰكَ مَا هِيَهۡ ١٠
Nārun Ĥāmiyah(tun)	(11) It is a Fire, intensely hot.	نَارٌ حَامِيَةُۢ ١١

سورة التكاثر

THE RIVALRY IN WORLD INCREASE ١٠٢ At-Takathur

Bismi Al-Lahi Ar-Raĥmāni Ar-Raĥīmi	In the name of Allāh, the Entirely Merciful, the Especially Merciful.	بِسۡمِ ٱللَّهِ ٱلرَّحۡمَٰنِ ٱلرَّحِيمِ
'Alhākumu At-Takāthuru	(1) Competition in [worldly] increase diverts you	أَلۡهَىٰكُمُ ٱلتَّكَاثُرُ ١
Ĥattá Zurtumu Al-Maqābira	(2) Until you visit the graveyards.	حَتَّىٰ زُرۡتُمُ ٱلۡمَقَابِرَ ٢

Kallā Sawfa Ta`lamūna	(3) No! You are going to know.	كَلَّا سَوۡفَ تَعۡلَمُونَ ٣
Thumma Kallā Sawfa Ta`lamūna	(4) Then, no! You are going to know.	ثُمَّ كَلَّا سَوۡفَ تَعۡلَمُونَ ٤
Kallā Law Ta`lamūna `Ilma Al-Yaqīni	(5) No! If you only knew with knowledge of certainty...	كَلَّا لَوۡ تَعۡلَمُونَ عِلۡمَ ٱلۡيَقِينِ ٥
Latarawunna Al-Jaĥīma	(6) You will surely see the Hellfire.	لَتَرَوُنَّ ٱلۡجَحِيمَ ٦
Thumma Latarawunnahā `Ayna Al-Yaqīni	(7) Then you will surely see it with the eye of certainty.	ثُمَّ لَتَرَوُنَّهَا عَيۡنَ ٱلۡيَقِينِ ٧
Thumma Latus'alunna Yawma'idhin `Ani An-Na`īmi	(8) Then you will surely be asked that Day about pleasure.	ثُمَّ لَتُسۡـَٔلُنَّ يَوۡمَئِذٍ عَنِ ٱلنَّعِيمِ ٨

سورة العصر

THE DECLINING DAY ١٠٣ Al-'Asr

Bismi Al-Lahi Ar-Raĥmāni Ar-Raĥīmi	In the name of Allāh, the Entirely Merciful, the Especially Merciful.	بِسۡمِ ٱللَّهِ ٱلرَّحۡمَٰنِ ٱلرَّحِيمِ
Wa Al-`Aşri	(1) By time,	وَٱلۡعَصۡرِ ١
'Inna Al-'Insāna Lafī Khusrin	(2) Indeed, mankind is in loss,	إِنَّ ٱلۡإِنسَٰنَ لَفِي خُسۡرٍ ٢
'Illā Al-Ladhīna 'Āmanū Wa `Amilū Aş-Şāliĥāti Wa Tawāşaw Bil-Ĥaqqi Wa Tawāşaw Biş-Şabri	(3) Except for those who have believed and done righteous deeds and advised each other to truth and advised each other to patience.	إِلَّا ٱلَّذِينَ ءَامَنُواْ وَعَمِلُواْ ٱلصَّٰلِحَٰتِ وَتَوَاصَوۡاْ بِٱلۡحَقِّ وَتَوَاصَوۡاْ بِٱلصَّبۡرِ ٣

سورة الهمزة

THE TRADUCER ١٠٤ Al-Humazah

Bismi Al-Lahi Ar-Raĥmāni Ar-Raĥīmi	In the name of Allāh, the Entirely Merciful, the Especially Merciful.	بِسۡمِ ٱللَّهِ ٱلرَّحۡمَٰنِ ٱلرَّحِيمِ
Waylun Likulli Humazatin Lumazah(tin)	(1) Woe to every scorner and mocker	وَيۡلٞ لِّكُلِّ هُمَزَةٖ لُّمَزَةٍ ١

Al-Ladhī Jama`a Mālāan Wa `Addadahu	(2) Who collects wealth and [continuously] counts it.	ٱلَّذِى جَمَعَ مَالًا وَعَدَّدَهُۥ ٢
Yaĥsabu 'Anna Mālahu 'Akhladahu	(3) He thinks that his wealth will make him immortal.	يَحْسَبُ أَنَّ مَالَهُۥٓ أَخْلَدَهُۥ ٣
Kallā Layunbadhanna Fī Al-Ĥuţamah(ti)	(4) No! He will surely be thrown into the Crusher.	كَلَّا ۖ لَيُنۢبَذَنَّ فِى ٱلْحُطَمَةِ ٤
Wa Mā 'Adrāka Mā Al-Ĥuţamah(tu)	(5) And what can make you know what is the Crusher?	وَمَآ أَدْرَىٰكَ مَا ٱلْحُطَمَةُ ٥
Nāru Al-Lahi Al-Mūqadah(tu)	(6) It is the fire of Allāh, [eternally] fueled,	نَارُ ٱللَّهِ ٱلْمُوقَدَةُ ٦
Allatī Taţţali`u `Alá Al-'Af'idah(ti)	(7) Which mounts directed at the hearts.	ٱلَّتِى تَطَّلِعُ عَلَى ٱلْأَفْـِٔدَةِ ٧
'Innahā `Alayhim Mu'uşadah(tun)	(8) Indeed, it [i.e., Hellfire] will be closed down upon them	إِنَّهَا عَلَيْهِم مُّؤْصَدَةٌ ٨
Fī `Amadin Mumaddadah(tin)	(9) In extended columns.	فِى عَمَدٍ مُّمَدَّدَةٍۭ ٩

Bismi Al-Lahi Ar-Raĥmāni Ar-Raĥīmi	In the name of Allāh, the Entirely Merciful, the Especially Merciful.	بِسۡمِ ٱللَّهِ ٱلرَّحۡمَٰنِ ٱلرَّحِيمِ
'Alam Tará Kayfa Fa`ala Rabbuka Bi'aşĥābi Al-Fīli	(1) Have you not considered, [O Muḥammad], how your Lord dealt with the companions of the elephant?	أَلَمۡ تَرَ كَيۡفَ فَعَلَ رَبُّكَ بِأَصۡحَٰبِ ٱلۡفِيلِ ١
'Alam Yaj`al Kaydahum Fī Tađlīlin	(2) Did He not make their plan into misguidance?	أَلَمۡ يَجۡعَلۡ كَيۡدَهُمۡ فِي تَضۡلِيلٖ ٢
Wa 'Arsala `Alayhim Ţayrāan 'Abābīla	(3) And He sent against them birds in flocks,	وَأَرۡسَلَ عَلَيۡهِمۡ طَيۡرًا أَبَابِيلَ ٣
Tarmīhim Biĥijāratin Min Sijjīlin	(4) Striking them with stones of hard clay,	تَرۡمِيهِم بِحِجَارَةٖ مِّن سِجِّيلٖ ٤
Faja`alahum Ka`aşfin Ma'kūlin	(5) And He made them like eaten straw.	فَجَعَلَهُمۡ كَعَصۡفٖ مَّأۡكُولِۭ ٥

Bismi Al-Lahi Ar-Raĥmāni Ar-Raĥīmi	In the name of Allāh, the Entirely Merciful, the Especially Merciful.	بِسۡمِ ٱللَّهِ ٱلرَّحۡمَٰنِ ٱلرَّحِيمِ
Li'īlāfi Quraysh_in	(1) For the accustomed security of the Quraysh -	لِإِيلَٰفِ قُرَيۡشٍ ١
'Īlāfihim Riĥlata Ash-Shitā'i Wa Aş-Şayfi	(2) Their accustomed security [in] the caravan of winter and summer -	إِۦلَٰفِهِمۡ رِحۡلَةَ ٱلشِّتَآءِ وَٱلصَّيۡفِ ٢
Falya`budū Rabba Hādhā Al-Bayti	(3) Let them worship the Lord of this House,	فَلۡيَعۡبُدُواْ رَبَّ هَٰذَا ٱلۡبَيۡتِ ٣
Al-Ladhī 'Aţ`amahum Min Jū`in Wa 'Āmanahum Min Khawfin	(4) Who has fed them, [saving them] from hunger and made them safe, [saving them] from fear.	ٱلَّذِيٓ أَطۡعَمَهُم مِّن جُوعٖ وَءَامَنَهُم مِّنۡ خَوۡفِۭ ٤

Bismi Al-Lahi Ar-Raĥmāni Ar-Raĥīmi	In the name of Allāh, the Entirely Merciful, the Especially Merciful.	بِسۡمِ ٱللَّهِ ٱلرَّحۡمَٰنِ ٱلرَّحِيمِ
'Ara'ayta Al-Ladhī Yukadhdhibu Bid-Dīni	(1) Have you seen the one who denies the Recompense?	أَرَءَيۡتَ ٱلَّذِي يُكَذِّبُ بِٱلدِّينِ ١
Fadhālika Al-Ladhī Yadu``u Al-Yatīma	(2) For that is the one who drives away the orphan	فَذَٰلِكَ ٱلَّذِي يَدُعُّ ٱلۡيَتِيمَ ٢
Wa Lā Yaĥuđđu `Alá Ţa`āmi Al-Miskīni	(3) And does not encourage the feeding of the poor.	وَلَا يَحُضُّ عَلَىٰ طَعَامِ ٱلۡمِسۡكِينِ ٣
Fawaylun Lilmuşallīna	(4) So woe to those who pray	فَوَيۡلٞ لِّلۡمُصَلِّينَ ٤
Al-Ladhīna Hum `An Şalātihim Sāhūna	(5) [But] who are heedless of their prayer -	ٱلَّذِينَ هُمۡ عَن صَلَاتِهِمۡ سَاهُونَ ٥
Al-Ladhīna Hum Yurā'ūna	(6) Those who make show [of their deeds]	ٱلَّذِينَ هُمۡ يُرَآءُونَ ٦
Wa Yamna`ūna Al-Mā`ūna	(7) And withhold [simple] assistance.	وَيَمۡنَعُونَ ٱلۡمَاعُونَ ٧

Bismi Al-Lahi Ar-Raĥmāni Ar-Raĥīmi	In the name of Allāh, the Entirely Merciful, the Especially Merciful.	بِسۡمِ ٱللَّهِ ٱلرَّحۡمَٰنِ ٱلرَّحِيمِ
'Innā 'A`ţaynāka Al-Kawthara	(1) Indeed, We have granted you, [O Muḥammad], al-Kawthar.	إِنَّآ أَعۡطَيۡنَٰكَ ٱلۡكَوۡثَرَ ١
Faşalli Lirabbika Wa Anĥar	(2) So pray to your Lord and offer sacrifice [to Him alone].	فَصَلِّ لِرَبِّكَ وَٱنۡحَرۡ ٢
'Inna Shāni'aka Huwa Al-'Abtaru	(3) Indeed, your enemy is the one cut off.	إِنَّ شَانِئَكَ هُوَ ٱلۡأَبۡتَرُ ٣

Bismi Al-Lahi Ar-Raĥmāni Ar-Raĥīmi	In the name of Allāh, the Entirely Merciful, the Especially Merciful.	بِسۡمِ ٱللَّهِ ٱلرَّحۡمَٰنِ ٱلرَّحِيمِ
Qul Yā 'Ayyuhā Al-Kāfirūna	(1) Say, "O disbelievers,	قُلۡ يَٰٓأَيُّهَا ٱلۡكَٰفِرُونَ ١
Lā 'A`budu Mā Ta`budūna	(2) I do not worship what you worship.	لَآ أَعۡبُدُ مَا تَعۡبُدُونَ ٢
Wa Lā 'Antum `Ābidūna Mā 'A`budu	(3) Nor are you worshippers of what I worship.	وَلَآ أَنتُمۡ عَٰبِدُونَ مَآ أَعۡبُدُ ٣
Wa Lā 'Anā `Ābidun Mā `Abadttum	(4) Nor will I be a worshipper of what you worship.	وَلَآ أَنَا۠ عَابِدٞ مَّا عَبَدتُّمۡ ٤
Wa Lā 'Antum `Ābidūna Mā 'A`budu	(5) Nor will you be worshippers of what I worship.	وَلَآ أَنتُمۡ عَٰبِدُونَ مَآ أَعۡبُدُ ٥
Lakum Dīnukum Wa Liya Dīni	(6) For you is your religion, and for me is my religion."	لَكُمۡ دِينُكُمۡ وَلِيَ دِينِ ٦

Bismi Al-Lahi Ar-Raĥmāni Ar-Raĥīmi	In the name of Allāh, the Entirely Merciful, the Especially Merciful.	بِسۡمِ ٱللَّهِ ٱلرَّحۡمَٰنِ ٱلرَّحِيمِ
'Idhā Jā'a Naşru Al-Lahi Wa Al-Fatĥu	(1) When the victory of Allāh has come and the conquest,	إِذَا جَآءَ نَصۡرُ ٱللَّهِ وَٱلۡفَتۡحُ ١
Wa Ra'ayta An-Nāsa Yadkhulūna Fī Dīni Al-Lahi 'Afwājāan	(2) And you see the people entering into the religion of Allāh in multitudes,	وَرَأَيۡتَ ٱلنَّاسَ يَدۡخُلُونَ فِي دِينِ ٱللَّهِ أَفۡوَاجٗا ٢
Fasabbiĥ Biĥamdi Rabbika Wa Astaghfirhu 'Innahu Kāna Tawwābāan	(3) Then exalt [Him] with praise of your Lord and ask forgiveness of Him. Indeed, He is ever Accepting of Repentance.	فَسَبِّحۡ بِحَمۡدِ رَبِّكَ وَٱسۡتَغۡفِرۡهُۚ إِنَّهُۥ كَانَ تَوَّابَۢا ٣

Bismi Al-Lahi Ar-Raĥmāni Ar-Raĥīmi	In the name of Allāh, the Entirely Merciful, the Especially Merciful.	بِسۡمِ ٱللَّهِ ٱلرَّحۡمَٰنِ ٱلرَّحِيمِ
Tabbat Yadā 'Abī Lahabin Wa Tabba	(1) May the hands of Abū Lahab be ruined, and ruined is he.	تَبَّتۡ يَدَآ أَبِي لَهَبٖ وَتَبَّ ١
Mā 'Aghná `Anhu Māluhu Wa Mā Kasaba	(2) His wealth will not avail him or that which he gained.	مَآ أَغۡنَىٰ عَنۡهُ مَالُهُۥ وَمَا كَسَبَ ٢
Sayaşlá Nārāan Dhāta Lahabin	(3) He will [enter to] burn in a Fire of [blazing] flame	سَيَصۡلَىٰ نَارٗا ذَاتَ لَهَبٖ ٣
Wa Amra'atuhu Ĥammālata Al-Ĥaţabi	(4) And his wife [as well] - the carrier of firewood.	وَٱمۡرَأَتُهُۥ حَمَّالَةَ ٱلۡحَطَبِ ٤
Fī Jīdihā Ĥablun Min Masadin	(5) Around her neck is a rope of [twisted] fiber.	فِي جِيدِهَا حَبۡلٞ مِّن مَّسَدِۭ ٥

Bismi Al-Lahi Ar-Raĥmāni Ar-Raĥīmi	In the name of Allāh, the Entirely Merciful, the Especially Merciful.	بِسۡمِ ٱللَّهِ ٱلرَّحۡمَٰنِ ٱلرَّحِيمِ
Qul Huwa Al-Lahu 'Aĥadun	(1) Say, "He is Allāh, [who is] One,	قُلۡ هُوَ ٱللَّهُ أَحَدٌ ١
Alllahu Aş-Şamadu	(2) Allāh, the Eternal Refuge.	ٱللَّهُ ٱلصَّمَدُ ٢
Lam Yalid Wa Lam Yūlad	(3) He neither begets nor is born,	لَمۡ يَلِدۡ وَلَمۡ يُولَدۡ ٣
Walam Yakun Lahu Kufūan 'Aĥadun	(4) Nor is there to Him any equivalent."	وَلَمۡ يَكُن لَّهُۥ كُفُوًا أَحَدُۢ ٤

سورة الفلق

THE DAYBREAK (113) Al-Falaq

Bismi Al-Lahi Ar-Rahmāni Ar-Rahīmi	In the name of Allāh, the Entirely Merciful, the Especially Merciful.	بِسۡمِ ٱللَّهِ ٱلرَّحۡمَٰنِ ٱلرَّحِيمِ
Qul 'A`ūdhu Birabbi Al-Falaqi	(1) Say, "I seek refuge in the Lord of daybreak	قُلۡ أَعُوذُ بِرَبِّ ٱلۡفَلَقِ ١
Min Sharri Mā Khalaqa	(2) From the evil of that which He created	مِن شَرِّ مَا خَلَقَ ٢
Wa Min Sharri Ghāsiqin 'Idhā Waqaba	(3) And from the evil of darkness when it settles	وَمِن شَرِّ غَاسِقٍ إِذَا وَقَبَ ٣
Wa Min Sharri An-Naffāthāti Fī Al-`Uqadi	(4) And from the evil of the blowers in knots	وَمِن شَرِّ ٱلنَّفَّٰثَٰتِ فِي ٱلۡعُقَدِ ٤
Wa Min Sharri Ĥāsidin 'Idhā Ĥasada	(5) And from the evil of an envier when he envies."	وَمِن شَرِّ حَاسِدٍ إِذَا حَسَدَ ٥

سورة الناس

THE MANKIND (114) An-Nas

Bismi Al-Lahi Ar-Raĥmāni Ar-Raĥīmi	In the name of Allāh, the Entirely Merciful, the Especially Merciful.	بِسۡمِ ٱللَّهِ ٱلرَّحۡمَٰنِ ٱلرَّحِيمِ
Qul 'A`ūdhu Birabbi An-Nāsi	(1) Say, "I seek refuge in the Lord of mankind,	قُلۡ أَعُوذُ بِرَبِّ ٱلنَّاسِ ١
Maliki An-Nāsi	(2) The Sovereign of mankind,	مَلِكِ ٱلنَّاسِ ٢
'Ilahi An-Nāsi	(3) The God of mankind,	إِلَٰهِ ٱلنَّاسِ ٣
Min Sharri Al-Waswāsi Al-Khannāsi	(4) From the evil of the retreating whisperer -	مِن شَرِّ ٱلۡوَسۡوَاسِ ٱلۡخَنَّاسِ ٤
Al-Ladhī Yuwaswisu Fī Şudūri An-Nāsi	(5) Who whispers [evil] into the breasts of mankind -	ٱلَّذِي يُوَسۡوِسُ فِي صُدُورِ ٱلنَّاسِ ٥
Mina Al-Jinnati Wa An-Nāsi	(6) From among the jinn and mankind".	مِنَ ٱلۡجِنَّةِ وَٱلنَّاسِ ٦

Table of Contents

الفهرس

Surah (Chapter)	As-Surat	Page / الصفحة	السّورة
THE OPENER	Al-Fatihah	4	الفَاتِحَة
THE TIDINGS	An-Naba	5	النَّبَإ
THOSE WHO DRAG FORTH	An-Nazi'at	10	النَّازِعَات
HE FROWNED	'Abasa	16	عَبَسَ
THE OVERTHROWING	At-Takwir	21	التَّكْوِير
THE CLEAVING	Al-Infitar	25	الانفِطَار
THE DEFRAUDING	Al-Mutaffifin	27	المُطَفِّفِينَ
THE SUNDERING	Al-Inshiqaq	32	الانشِقَاق
THE MANSIONS OF THE STARS	Al-Buruj	35	البُرُوج
THE NIGHTCOMMER	At-Tariq	39	الطَّارِق
THE MOST HIGH	Al-A'la	41	الأَعْلَى
THE OVERWHELMING	Al-Ghashiyah	43	الغَاشِيَة
THE DAWN	Al-Fajr	46	الفَجْر
THE CITY	Al-Balad	50	البَلَد
THE SUN	Ash-Shams	52	الشَّمْس
THE NIGHT	Al-Layl	55	اللَّيْل
THE MORNING HOURS	Ad-Duhaa	57	الضُّحَى
THE RELIEF	Ash-Sharh	58	الشَّرْح
THE FIG	At-Tin	59	التِّين
THE CLOT	Al-'Alaq	61	العَلَق
THE POWER	Al-Qadr	63	القَدْر

THE CLEAR PROOF	Al-Bayyinah	64	البَيِّنَة
THE EARTHQUAKE	Az-Zalzalah	66	الزَّلْزَلَة
THE COURSER	Al-'Adiyat	67	العَادِيَات
THE CALAMITY	Al-Qari'ah	69	القَارِعَة
THE RIVALRY IN WORLD INCREASE	At-Takathur	70	التَّكَاثُر
THE DECLINING DAY	Al-'Asr	72	العَصْر
THE TRADUCER	Al-Humazah	72	الهُمَزَة
THE ELEPHANT	Al-Fil	74	الفِيل
QURAYSH	Quraysh	75	قُرَيْش
THE SMALL KINDESSES	Al-Ma'un	76	المَاعُون
THE ABUNDANCE	Al-Kawthar	77	الكَوْثَر
THE DISBELIEVERS	Al-Kafirun	78	الكَافِرُونَ
THE DIVINE SUPPORT	An-Nasr	79	النَّصْر
THE PALM FIBER	Al-Masad	80	المَسَد
THE SINCERITY	Al-Ikhlas	81	الإِخْلَاص
THE DAYBREAK	Al-Falaq	82	الفَلَق
THE MANKIND	An-Nas	83	النَّاس

Made in United States
North Haven, CT
01 September 2025

72339568R00050